The Mythological Cycle of Medieval Irish Literature

John Carey

Cork Studies in Celtic Literatures 3

2018

for Nita

isind oceon frinn aníar

Cork Studies in Celtic Literatures 3

The Mythological Cycle of Medieval Irish Literature

John Carey

2018

www.ucc.ie/en/cscl

Published by Cork Studies in Celtic Literatures

ISBN: 978-0-9955469-2-9

Published with the assistance of University College Cork's

CACSSS Research Publication Fund

Contents

	Abbreviations	i
	Preface	ii
1	The 'Cycles' of Medieval Irish Literature	1
2	Who Are the Túatha Dé?	9
3	Tales Related to *Táin Bó Cúailnge*	19
4	Further Old Irish Tales	29
5	Lore and Fantasy in the Middle Irish Period	38
6	The Later Tradition	49
7	Conclusion	59
	Bibliography	60
	General Index	71
	Index of Manuscripts	76
	Index of Scholars	77

Abbreviations

ATU	Aarne-Thompson-Uther tale type
BL	British Library, London
CLH	*Clavis Litterarum Hibernensium*; D. Ó Corráin
CMCS	*Cambridge/Cambrian Medieval Celtic Studies*
DIL	*Dictionary of the Irish Language*; E.G. Quin (gen. ed.)
ÉC	*Études celtiques*
ITS	Irish Texts Society
LL	*The Book of Leinster*; R.I. Best et al.
LU	*Lebor na hUidre*; R.I. Best and O. Bergin
MD	*The Metrical Dindshenchas*; E.J. Gwynn
MMIS	Mediaeval and Modern Irish Series
NLI	National Library of Ireland, Dublin
PHCC	*Proceedings of the Harvard Celtic Colloquium*
RC	*Revue celtique*
RIA	Royal Irish Academy, Dublin
TCD	Trinity College Dublin
UCD-OFM	University College Dublin, Franciscan Collection
ZCP	*Zeitschrift für celtische Philologie*

Preface

Since the late nineteenth century, several medieval Irish tales have been regarded as constituting a 'mythological cycle'; and while it is recognised that this category is the creation of modern scholarship, it is nevertheless widely accepted as designating a significant grouping in the literature. Investigators of the religious beliefs of the pre-Christian Celtic peoples have often regarded these stories as a particularly valuable body of evidence, as if they were indeed in some sense representative of 'Celtic mythology'.

This study has two aims: to examine the background and validity of the concept of an 'Irish mythological cycle'; and to provide an overview of the texts that have been — and that can be — included under such a heading. Even if the medieval Irish did not think in these terms (and would, perhaps, have been disconcerted or indignant had anyone told them that they were producing 'mythological' narratives), they were certainly preoccupied with the enigmatic beings who are the protagonists of these tales. Considering the texts as a group can further our understanding of an important aspect of the mental world that lies behind the literature.

It will be evident from this book's modest size that there are many important topics, closely related to the present enquiry, which have not been examined. Save tangentially, I have not offered any conjectures concerning the narratives that presumably formed part of the religious culture of the pre-Christian forebears of the medieval Irish: the real 'Celtic mythology' which, however many traces and reflections it may have left in the literatures of the Celtic peoples and their neighbours, is lost to us forever. In considering the medieval evidence, moreover, I have been concerned primarily with surveying the tales as tales, rather than with giving accounts of such elements within them as the 'Otherworld' or realm of the *síde*,[1] or the portrayal of individual characters.[2] I have

[1] Discussions include Ó Cathasaigh, 'The Semantics of *Síd*'; Carey, 'The Location of the Otherworld'; idem, 'Time, Space, and the Otherworld'; idem, 'Ireland and the Antipodes'; idem, 'Otherworlds and Verbal Worlds'; idem, 'The Irish "Otherworld"'; Sims-Williams, *Irish Influence*, 53–78; Sayers, 'Netherworld and Otherworld'; Mac Mathúna, 'The Relationship of the Chthonic World'.

[2] As examples of work in this area may be mentioned Lehmacher, 'Der Dagde'; Carey, 'Nodons in Britain and Ireland'; Dagger, 'Eithne: The Sources'; MacQuarrie, *The Biography of the Irish God of the Sea*; Egeler, *Walküren, Bodbs, Sirenen*; Carey, 'Ogmios and the Eternal Word'.

however dedicated Chapter Two to a discussion of the nature of the *Túath(a) Dé* ('Tribe(s) of Gods'), the supernatural race at the heart of the 'mythological cycle': in examining a body of material usually defined with reference to these beings, it would be impossible to proceed without some sense of who they were thought to be.

This enquiry was first undertaken several years ago, as part of a larger collaborative project which did not reach fruition. I am grateful to Kevin Murray for encouraging me to return to my initial effort, and to expand and update it for inclusion in this series.[3] I am further grateful to him, and to the book's two anonymous readers, for many observations and suggestions: these have added to what the book has to offer, as well as ameliorating its shortcomings. I remain, of course, solely responsible for all flaws that remain.

[3] Two recent publications in particular have contributed fundamentally to this book in its final form: Mark Williams's *Ireland's Immortals*, a study of the Túatha Dé of unprecedented breadth and richness; and the late Donnchadh Ó Corráin's epochal *Clavis Litterarum Hibernensium* (cited as *CLH* below), to which all future students of medieval Irish literature will be indebted.

1. The 'Cycles' of Medieval Irish Literature

How has it come about that those studying medieval Irish literature think in terms of a 'mythological cycle' — a term that, arguably, has no close counterpart elsewhere in European literary studies? The phrase, now in general use, was first formulated late in the nineteenth century.

Following his retirement, at the age of fifty-three, from the post of director of the archives of the department of Aube, Henri d'Arbois de Jubainville was commissioned by Jules Ferry, the Minister of Public Education and the Fine Arts, to undertake a 'mission littéraire' to England and Ireland; the purpose of this expedition was 'to prepare a catalogue of Irish manuscripts, and to study the Celtic antiquities of Ireland'.[1] He carried out his task in the summer of 1882, the same year in which he became the first occupant of the chair of Celtic language and literature at the Collège de France; and the catalogue was published in 1883.[2] He had already launched the seminal 'Cours de littérature celtique', and his own initial contributions to this series reflect his aim to gain a comprehensive overview of medieval Irish literature, and especially of Irish legendary narrative. In the first volume, *Introduction à l'étude de la littérature celtique*, he offered the following characterisation of the narrative corpus as a whole:

> The epic literature of Ireland is composed of a great number of fragments, of very unequal length, of which the earliest are generally written in prose, but with an admixture of verse, and which for the most part belong to three cycles: the first cycle is the mythological cycle, which has as its object the origin of the gods and of men; the second is the heroic cycle of Conchobar and Cú Chulainn [...]. The third cycle has as its principal subject the exploits of Finn and Oisín, chiefs of the national militia of Ireland, and a sort of fabulous history of Ireland when these two personages appear to have lived, that is, in the second or third century of our era. In this cycle, as in that preceding, it is difficult always to be certain of the precise point where reality ends and fiction begins. Besides these three great cycles, Irish epic literature includes certain fragments relating to subsequent events.[3]

[1] Arbois de Jubainville, 'Rapport sur une mission littéraire', 141.

[2] *Essai d'un catalogue.*

[3] *Introduction à l'étude de la littérature celtique*, 44–5: 'La littérature épique de l'Irlande se compose d'un grand nombre de morceaux, de longueurs très

These categories were readily adopted by other scholars. In his 1913 *Bibliography of Irish Philology and of Printed Irish Literature*, R.I. Best noted that 'the traditional Irish classification of these tales is by titles, into Battles, Courtships, Destructions, Tragic Deaths, etc.'; but he preferred to this 'disconnected arrangement' a system under the headings 'Mythological and Tuatha De Danann Cycle', 'Conchobar-Cuchullin Cycle', 'Finn or Ossianic Cycle' and 'Other Cycles'.[4] A further development to the system appears to have been introduced by Myles Dillon. Writing in 1946, he observed of the tales relating to kings that 'these "historical" tales may be grouped into cycles around the names of the kings who appear in them', but also spoke of 'the four cycles of Irish sagas', as if all such tales of kings could be grouped into a single cycle: Arbois de Jubainville's 'certain fragments relating to subsequent events' now comprised another primary category.[5] Two decades later, in the chapter on Irish literature that he contributed to *The Celtic Realms*, Dillon referred explicitly to 'the Cycle of the Kings'.[6]

The convenient fourfold grouping thus arrived at has been widely employed in subsequent scholarship;[7] but there have been occasional moves to expand it further. Thus Gerard Murphy advocated five categories: 'Modern scholars [...] prefer to classify the stories partly according to their subject-matter and partly

---

inégales, dont les plus anciens sont ordinairement écrits en prose, mais avec mélange de vers, et qui pour la plupart appartiennent à trois cycles: le premier cycle est le cycle mythologique, qui a pour objet l'origine des dieux et des hommes; le second est le cycle héroïque de Conchobar et de Cùchulainn [...]. Le troisième cycle a pour sujet principal les exploits de Finn et d'Ossin, chefs de la milice nationale d'Irlande, et une sorte d'histoire fabuleuse de l'Irlande à l'époque où paraissent avoir vécu ces deux personnages, c'est-à-dire au second et au troisième siècle de notre ère. Dans ce cycle, comme dans le précédent, il est difficile de distinguer toujours avec certitude le point précis où finit la réalité et où commence la fiction. Outre ces trois grands cycles, la littérature épique irlandaise comprend quelques morceaux relatifs à des évènements postérieurs'.

[4] *Bibliography of Irish Philology* [...] *to 1912*, pp. v, x.

[5] *The Cycles of the Kings*, pp. v, 2.

[6] Dillon and Chadwick, *The Celtic Realms*, 240.

[7] Thus Williams and Ford, *The Irish Literary Tradition*, 126. Muireann Ní Bhrolcháin acknowledged the varying attitudes to the classification of the king tales when she observed that 'this Cycle is really a composite one' (*An Introduction to Early Irish Literature*, 67). Dan M. Wiley similarly speaks of 'the so-called Historical Cycle, otherwise known as the Cycles of the Kings' ('An Introduction to the Early Irish King Tales', 15).

according to their spirit into Mythological tales, Heroic tales, King tales, Finn tales, and Romantic tales'.[8] Thinking more broadly still, Tomás Ó Cathasaigh has proposed that 'we can probably speak of the Cycles of the Saints, and when the material on the poets has been studied it may be that Cycles of the Poets will be identified'.[9] But this is not the place for attempting an overview of all of the opinions on this many-sided question.[10]

While it is recognised that these cycles are an academic construct,[11] their neatness and usefulness can be seductive: thus the brothers Alwyn and Brinley Rees suggested that the cycles could be correlated with the provinces of Ireland, and went on to assert that 'the ancient storytellers were doubtless aware of these separate "cycles", each with its distinct *dramatis personae*', even though 'there is no mention of them as such in the extant literature'.[12] For his part, Kuno Meyer suggested that tales of the mythological cycle, in particular, take the reader back to 'Common Celtic times'.[13]

Not only do we owe to Arbois de Jubainville the fourfold scheme of which the 'mythological cycle' forms a part, but he was also the first to devote to that cycle an extended study: this was his book *Le cycle mythologique irlandais et la mythologie celtique*, published in 1884. Here he discussed the medieval Irish tale-lists, with their very different approach to organising the narrative corpus, before going on to state that 'the monuments of Irish epic literature seem to fall naturally into four sections'. Of these, he described the mythological cycle as that 'which deals with the origin of the world and the most ancient history of the gods and of

---

[8] *Saga and Myth*, 13.

[9] '*Cath Maige Tuired* as Exemplary Myth', 18 n. 63.

[10] An extended study of the modern taxonomy of Celtic narrative, placing the matters discussed here in a broader historical and theoretical context, is Poppe, *Of Cycles and Other Critical Matters*. Poppe discusses the background of 'cycle' as a literary term (pp. 3–5), mentions Arbois de Jubainville (p. 5), and provides a useful table of variations on his scheme of cycles (p. 13).

[11] For example, Dillon: 'There is no tradition in favour of this arrangement' (*The Cycles of the Kings*, 3); 'The classification into cycles is modern' (*Early Irish Literature*, 1). Herbert likewise speaks of the cycles as a 'modern categorization of the literary corpus' ('*Fled Dúin na nGéd*: A Reappraisal', 76).

[12] *Celtic Heritage*, 123–4, 207.

[13] 'Noch in gemeinkeltische Zeiten und Überlieferung führt uns zunächst in seinen ältesten Bestandteilen der mythologische Sagenkreis zurück' ('Die irisch-gälische Literatur', 82–3).

men'.[14]

Not all of the elements in Arbois de Jubainville's system lack a traditional basis. Stories about Find and his *fían* are clearly a distinct native category, designated by the term *fíanaigecht* (modern *fiannaíocht*) from the beginning of the Early Modern period onward;[15] this may well also be the sense of the phrase *fíanṡruth Find*, literally '*fían*-stream of Find', that is already found in a list of entertainments in a poem composed in the eleventh century.[16] Similarly, the various tales about the adventures of Cú Chulainn and his fellow Ulaid warriors share a cast of characters, and are set in a more or less coherent narrative world. A term *rudhraigheacht* or *rúraíocht*, derived from the name of the legendary Ulaid ancestor Rudraige mac Sittride, appears to have been used as a collective term for such tales since at least the sixteenth century.[17] Tales concerning individual kings, too, have an obvious shared reference.

But where in Old, Middle or Modern Irish literature could one expect to find tales dealing with 'the origin of the world and the most ancient history of the gods and of men'? A medieval European would turn to the book of Genesis, not to 'epic literature', for an account of the origins of the world and of mankind; and, although we will see below that a strong case can be made for calling the supernatural beings of Irish legend 'gods', it is by no means clear that we are entitled to view the narratives in which they figure as being 'myths' in any significant sense.[18]

In his exploration of the 'mythological cycle', Arbois de Jubainville took as his principal source the account of Ireland's early settlements in the pseudo-historical treatise *Lebor Gabála Érenn* ('The Book of the Taking of Ireland'), more specifically the

[14] I cite the translation by R.I. Best: *The Irish Mythological Cycle*, 2. In the original, Arbois de Jubainville refers to 'le cycle mythologique, qui concerne l'origine et la plus ancienne histoire des dieux, des hommes et du monde' (*Le cycle mythologique irlandais*, 4).

[15] The earliest example noted in *DIL* s.v. '**fíanaigecht** [...] (**b**) *fían-lore, (telling) stories of the fíana*' is in *Acallam na Senórach*: Stokes, 'Acallamh na Senórach', l. 6526. The term's emergence is discussed in detail by Joseph Flahive in a forthcoming article.

[16] *MD* iii, 20. E.J. Gwynn, the editor, tentatively proposed for the poem a specific date of A.D. 1079 (p. 471).

[17] Thus Dinneen, *Foclóir Gaedhilge agus Béarla*, s.v. The word is already used in the more general sense 'idle tale' in a poem composed in A.D. 1600: Ó Murchú, 'D'Uaithne Ó Mórdha', 346 l. 28.

[18] In some cases it is however possible to argue that such tales may derive from earlier myths; see pp. 7, n. 28 and 36, n. 31 below.

version of that text which is preserved in the Book of Leinster (TCD MS 1339; shelfmark H 2.18): he believed this to reflect the lost *tochomlada*, or stories of migrations, which are mentioned in the Middle Irish tale-lists. In his own detailed analysis of these lists, however, Proinsias Mac Cana subsequently argued that the situation was more or less the reverse of what Arbois de Jubainville had supposed, with the *tochomlada* in question bearing titles 'drawn from *Lebor Gabála*', and representing 'an advanced stage in the elaboration of the *L*[*ebor*] *G*[*abála*] synthesis'.[19]

But there is a more fundamental difficulty with Arbois de Jubainville's approach. *Lebor Gabála Érenn*, and all of the other Irish pseudo-historical texts that have come down to us, represent not native mythology as such but rather a euhemeristic attempt to find a place for Ireland, and for its people, within the vision of the past that Christian scholars had elaborated on the basis of the Bible.[20] In assigning *Lebor Gabála Érenn*, and a handful of related tales, to his 'mythological cycle', Arbois was accordingly thinking not of the texts themselves but of *lost pagan traditions which he believed to lie behind them*.[21] This places the first of his cycles on a plane entirely different from that of the other three. It is defined not in terms of *what it is* but of *what it may once have been*: to speak bluntly, it is not valid as a descriptive category. If we are to use the term 'mythological cycle' at all, therefore, we must find a way of doing so with reference to the medieval literature in which the tales are found — not in terms of an antecedent oral tradition, whose contents must remain a matter of conjecture.

In the section devoted to the 'mythological cycle' in the first volume of Best's *Bibliography*, considerable space is accorded to the medieval *Dindṡenchas* collections, assemblages of legends accounting for the origins of placenames; in the second volume, however, treatment of this material has been shifted to the category 'Miscellaneous: Topographical'.[22] Best's early choice is

---

[19] Mac Cana, *The Learned Tales*, 116.

[20] Euhemerism has been defined as a type of 'mythological interpretation which supposes certain gods ... to be originally heroes' (Rose and Hornblower, 'Euhemerus'). For some observations on the role of euhemerism in Irish thought, see Carey, *A Single Ray of the Sun*, 14–20.

[21] Cf. my remarks in Carey, 'New Introduction', [7].

[22] Best, *Bibliography of Irish Philology* [...] *to 1912*, 80–82; *Bibliography of Irish Philology* [...] *1913–1941*, 179–80. Cf. the section 'Onomastic Lore' in Baumgarten, *Bibliography of Irish Linguistics and Literature 1942–71*, 560–61. I follow Downey, 'Cúán ua Lothcháin and the Transmission of the *Dindṡenchas*', 45 n. 1, in using *dindṡenchas* as the Irish term for 'placename lore' in general; capitalised *Dindṡenchas* refers to a collection of texts

understandable: there is an obvious sense in which *dindṡenchas* anecdotes can be seen as relating to 'the origin and the most ancient history of [...] the world'.[23] Indeed, many of them have as their protagonists the immortal people of the *síde*, and these will be discussed in more detail below. But the primary focus of *dindṡenchas* is onomastic, not 'mythological', and it draws its tales from every part of the narrative tradition. If we treat such a genre as 'mythology', simply because some items within it go back (or so at least it is argued) to earlier myths, then we can equally well include a glossary such as *Sanas Cormaic*.[24]

The tale *Tochmarc Étaíne* is usually regarded as one of the most prominent representatives of the 'mythological cycle',[25] but even here there are problems. Of the story's three sections, two are set in the reign of Eochaid Airem, a mortal king of Tara one of whose brothers was an ancestor of the kings of Connacht and of the dynasties of the Uí Néill. Moreover, one of the narrative's main functions is to indicate the background of the disasters which later overtook the ill-starred ruler Conaire Már, whose death ushered in that hiatus in the legendary over-kingship of Ireland which is part of the background of the events recounted in the 'Ulster cycle'; as a matter of fact, stories about Eochaid Airem and Étaín are elsewhere described as *remscéla* or 'fore-tales' for the account of Conaire's downfall.[26] Far from having primordial events in the realm of the gods as its focus, therefore, *Tochmarc Étaíne* is concerned with providing a context for some of the principal exploits of Irish heroic saga.

Without further belabouring the point, I think that there are grounds for the view that the label 'mythological cycle' is, in the end, more trouble than it is worth.[27] It can certainly be argued,

---

concerned with such lore.

[23] This circumstance indeed led Marie-Louise Sjoestedt to refer to *dindṡenchas* as 'the Irish myth of place' ('le mythe topique irlandais': *Dieux et héros des Celtes*, 34).

[24] See discussion below, p. 16.

[25] Thus Dillon, while acknowledging that 'the mythological cycle is not well represented in the literature', considered *Tochmarc Étaíne* to be 'one of [its] two principal surviving tales': *Early Irish Literature*, 51, 54. Arbois de Jubainville had already given the tale a prominent place in his own survey: *The Irish Mythological Cycle*, 176–82. See below, pp. 29–31.

[26] *LU* ll. 8007–9; cf. Carey, 'On the Interrelationships', 89–90. This point will be further discussed below, in connection not only with *Tochmarc Étaíne* but with other tales as well.

[27] For other objections to the term, based on a more flexible use of the word 'myth' than that adopted here, see Ó Cathasaigh, '*Cath Maige Tuired*', 11.

sometimes persuasively so, that elements in this or that medieval Irish tale reflect an earlier myth;[28] but this cannot be the basis for a synchronic taxonomy. Myles Dillon attempted an alternative definition, framed within the terms of the medieval tradition itself, when he proposed that the mythological cycle deals 'with heroes who were thought to have lived in Ireland before the coming of the Gaels'.[29] But apart from certain items in the *Dindṡenchas* collections, parts of *Lebor Gabála Érenn*, and the unusual tale *Cath Maige Tuired*, there is very little that can properly be assigned to such a category. Gregory Toner's characterisation is more satisfactory, while at the same time reflecting the arbitrary nature of the 'cycle':

> The Mythological Cycle is that body of medieval Irish narrative literature chiefly concerned with the deeds of the inhabitants of the Irish otherworld. Characters from this cycle frequently appear in the other three main cycles (the Ulster Cycle, the King Cycle, and the Finn Cycle) as well as in other categories of narrative that fall outside this classification such as the *dinnsenchas* ('place-lore').[30]

In describing the literature which has come down to us, it would seem better to speak simply of stories (not a 'cycle') concerning the Túatha Dé, Túatha Dé Donann[31] or 'people of the *síde*' — beings whose ambiguous nature will be discussed in the following chapter.

What tales we assign to this category will be, to a great extent, a matter of individual judgement.[32] There will obviously be

---

Ó Cathasaigh suggests that 'a happier choice of title would be the Cycle — or Cycles — of the Gods'. This position has been restated by Wiley, who concedes however that the 'current name is so well established that it is unlikely to be changed' ('Mythological Cycle', 1326).

[28] I have made some suggestions along these lines: for example, 'Nōdons, Lugus, Windos'; 'Donn, Amairgen, Íth'.

[29] *Irish Sagas*, 12; he went on however to opine that this material is 'the chief source of knowledge of the religion of the pagan Irish'.

[30] 'Mythological Cycle', 348.

[31] This name usually appears as 'Túatha Dé Danann' in the secondary literature. But *Danann* is a later form of *Donann*, and is apparently first attested (and there only occasionally) in the Book of Leinster; discussion in Carey, 'The Name "Tuatha Dé Danann"'.

[32] The difficulties involved have of course been widely recognised. Thus Rudolf Thurneysen, while assigning the main subject matter of the 'mythologische Sagenkreis' to the 'Urgeschichte Irlands', acknowledged:

no uncertainty when all of the characters belong to the Túatha Dé; and it has been generally accepted that stories involving mortals, in which the central figure or figures are of the Túatha Dé, should be included also. But how are we to regard tales in which a mortal hero has a supernatural encounter, such as *Airne Fíngein* ('The Night-Watch of Fíngen');[33] or accounts of such a hero's adventures in the realm of the *síde*, such as *Baile in Scáil* ('The Trance of the Phantom') or *Serglige Con Culainn* ('The Wasting Sickness of Cú Chulainn')?[34] What of the Otherworld journey tales called *echtrai* and *immrama*?[35] I have not felt able to treat such stories here,[36] but I readily acknowledge that an argument could be made for their inclusion. I shall also not be looking at stories in which one or another of the Túatha Dé makes only a cameo appearance, as is the case for Lug in *Táin Bó Cúailnge* ('The Cattle Raid of Cúailnge'),[37] for Manannán in *Compert Mongáin* ('The Conception of Mongán'),[38] for Óengus in tales of the hero Díarmait ua Duibne,[39] and for the Dagda in *Mesca Ulad* ('The Intoxication of the Ulaid').[40] The inevitability of disagreement on such questions should be regarded as an advantage rather than as a drawback: it can serve to remind us that we are dealing, not with a concept intrinsic to the tradition itself, but with a classification created to accommodate the interests and convenience of later scholarship.

'Aber natürlich kommen die überirdischen Wesen (Elfen und Feen) in Texten jeder Art vor' (*Die irische Helden- und Königsage*, 5).

33 Vendryes, *Airne Fíngein*.

34 Murray, *Baile in Scáil*; Dillon, *Serglige Con Culainn*.

35 While *immrama* are tales of voyages overseas, and most *echtrai* are not, these terms do not appear to be mutually exclusive in any strict sense. Attempts at definition made by Dumville, '*Echtrae* and *Immram*' and Mac Mathúna, *Immram Brain*, 248–85 have been criticised by Breatnach, 'Review', 188 and McCone, *Echtrae Chonnlai*, 64–7. See further Duignan, *The Echtrae*; Wooding, *The Otherworld Voyage*.

36 I have made an exception in the case of *Echtra Nerai*, as it seems to have close links with other early tales concerning the Túatha Dé; see discussion below, pp. 24–7.

37 O'Rahilly, *Táin Bó Cúailnge*, 64–5.

38 White, *Compert Mongáin*, 71–2, 78–9.

39 Besides Óengus's role in *Tóruigheacht Dhiarmada agus Ghráinne*, there is an earlier instance of his functioning as a *deus ex machina* for Díarmait in Meyer, 'Uath Beinne Etair'.

40 Watson, *Mesca Ulad*, 28. These four examples are only illustrative; a full list of such more or less brief apparitions in the literature would be a long one.

2. Who Are the Túatha Dé?

Before considering the tales themselves, we must give some attention to the figures who are their principal protagonists. What evidence do we have of their original nature as gods — an identification which is the main reason that the stories concerning them have been called 'mythological'? And if they were indeed gods at first, to what extent was their divinity remembered in the medieval period? Was there any lingering belief in their possession of supernatural powers? Or, if they were not held to be gods, what sort of beings did medieval writers conceive them to be; and how are they imagined in the stories in which they appear?

The Irish word *síd* designates a height of land — either a natural hill or mountain, or an artificial mound — thought to be the dwelling place of supernatural beings, or to be a point of entry into a supernatural realm. Its earliest surviving attestation may be in a famous passage in Tírechán's *Collectanea*, an account of Saint Patrick's mission to Ireland written late in the seventh century: here two princesses, seeing the saint and his followers for the first time and not knowing what to make of them, imagine that they are 'men of the *síde*, or of the earthly gods, or an apparition' (*uiros side aut deorum terrenorum aut fantassiam*).[1] With few exceptions,[2] these words have been taken to indicate that the people of the *síde* were the gods of the pagan Irish, 'earthly' by distinction from the one God of heaven.[3] The same conception appears to be reflected in a hymn in honour of Patrick, generally regarded as an Old Irish composition, which includes the statement 'the tribes used to worship the *síde*' (*tūatha adortais síde*);[4] and it presumably also underlies the designations *Túath(a) Dé* ('Tribe(s)

---

[1] Bieler, *The Patrician Texts*, 142.

[2] Draak, *Schimmen van het wester-eiland*, 27–8, held that 'men of the *síde*' and '(men of) the earthly gods' in this passage are to be taken as alternatives, not as equivalents. For an account of her views, I am dependent on Borsje, 'Monotheistic to a Certain Extent', 58. Another perspective on the *dei terreni* is offered by Maier, 'Dead Men Don't Wear Plaid', 113–14.

[3] On the ambiguity of the Latin, see now Williams, *Ireland's Immortals*, 40–41. For other early Irish texts that distinguish between God in heaven and gods on earth, see Carey, 'From David to Labraid'; for the use of a by-form *dee* as a term for pagan divinities specifically, see idem, '*Dee* "Pagan Deity"'.

[4] Stokes and Strachan, *Thesaurus Palaeohibernicus*, ii, 317. Another possible translation of the line is 'they [the "folk of Ireland" mentioned in the preceding line] used to worship the tribes of the *síde*'.

of Gods') and the rarer *Fir Dé* ('Men of Gods'), and the name of the *síd* overlord called the *Dagda* (from *dag* 'good' + *día* 'god').[5] That the Túatha Dé of medieval legend are in fact derived from the divinities of the pre-Christian Irish is confirmed by the presence among their number of figures corresponding to gods attested elsewhere in the Celtic world: the most straight-forward instances are *Lug* (cf. Continental Celtic *Lugus*),[6] *Ogma* (cf. Continental Celtic *Ogmios*),[7] and *Núadu* (cf. British *Nōdons*).[8]

Mention should also be made here of a group of supernatural beings called *Fomoiri*.[9] These appear in the tale *Cath Maige Tuired* as a race distinct from, and throughout most of the narrative opposed to, the Túatha Dé; and in *Lebor Gabála Érenn* they are portrayed as invaders, contending against the Túatha Dé and also against the earlier settlements of Ireland led by Partholón and Nemed. This polarised depiction, in two such prominent texts, has led to a perception of the two groups as being antithetical in essence: thus Arbois de Jubainville compared their antagonism to that of gods and Titans in Greek mythology, and of *devas* and

---

[5] This etymology, which there is no reason not to regard as the correct one, is attested in the medieval Irish sources themselves; thus it is already implicit in *Tochmarc Étaíne*, where it is said of him that he was called *Dagda* because 'it was he who used to work miracles, and to apportion storms and fruits for them' (*ba hé dognith na firta ⁊ conmidhedh na sina ⁊ na toirthe doib*; Bergin and Best, 'Tochmarc Étaíne', 142). Mark Williams observes that the Dagda is here 'described in the most explicitly godlike terms found in any Irish saga' (*Ireland's Immortals*, 86–7). Eric Hamp has proposed the alternative sense 'god of the good ones', i.e. of the nobility ('The Dag(h)d(h)ae and his Relatives', 166); further discussion in Blažek, 'Celto-Slavic Parallels', 75–7.

[6] See, for example, the discussions in Tovar, 'The God *Lugus* in Spain'; Carey, 'Eine keltische Schicksalsgöttin?'.

[7] Carey, 'Ogmios and the Eternal Word'.

[8] Carey, 'Nodons in Britain and Ireland'. Another instance appears to be *Brigit*, one of the Túatha Dé who is called a 'goddess' (*dea*) in *Sanas Cormaic* (§150) and whose name is cognate with that of the British tutelary goddess who was Romanised as *Brigantia*. But here the case is complicated by ongoing scholarly disagreement regarding the possible presence of pagan elements in traditions concerning Saint Brigit of Kildare; discussion in McKenna, 'Apotheosis and Evanescence'.

[9] While Meyer followed the early medieval view that the second element in the name is the word *muir* 'sea' ('Zur keltischen Wortkunde V', 635; cf. the equation *na muiride .i. na Fomorach* in van Hamel, *Lebor Bretnach*, 21), Thurneysen proposed that it in fact goes back to a root **mor-* 'goblin, demon', from which the element 'mare' in English 'nightmare' is also derived (*Die irische Helden- und Königsage*, 64; cf. Pokorny, *Indogermanisches etymologisches Wörterbuch*, 736).

asuras in India, with Georges Dumézil making a further comparison with the *Æsir* and *Vanir* of Scandinavia.[10] In works with no obvious dependence on *Cath Maige Tuired* and *Lebor Gabála Érenn*, however, the picture is not so clear-cut. The Fomoiri may appear as ferocious (sometimes monstrous) beings from beyond the sea, but without a stated relationship, positive or negative, with the Túatha Dé. A particularly striking example along these lines occurs in the tale *Togail Bruidne Da Derga* ('The Destruction of Da Derga's Hostel').[11] On the other hand, even *Cath Maige Tuired* and *Lebor Gabála Érenn* seem sometimes to suggest the absence of a clear distinction between Fomoiri and Túatha Dé: in *Cath Maige Tuired* the 'sons of Tethra' ([...] *maccu Tethra*), a term clearly intended to designate the Fomoiri, are spoken of as residing in the *síde* (*hi sídaib*);[12] and *Lebor Gabála Érenn* speaks at one point of 'demons and Fomoiri, that is [...] the Túatha Dé Donann'.[13] Even in the later Middle Ages, the Fenian tale *Tóruigheacht Dhiarmada agus Ghráinne* ('The Pursuit of Díarmait and Gráinne') identifies an ogre of the Fomoiri as a warrior of the Túatha Dé.[14] Given this ambiguity, it would seem best to describe the Fomoiri simply as supernatural beings who are almost invariably sinister, and whose identity overlaps in some sources to a greater or lesser extent with that of the Túatha Dé.[15]

There are indications that the Túatha Dé were not merely characters in narrative, but were at least to some extent also the

---

[10] Arbois de Jubainville, *The Irish Mythological Cycle*, 7; Dumézil, *Mythe et épopée*, i, 288–90; but see Sayers, 'Bargaining for the Life of Bres'. Cf. p. 36, n. 30 below.

[11] Knott, *Togail Bruidne Da Derga*, 27–8.

[12] Gray, *Cath Maige Tuired*, 48, l. 447. Similarly, in the tale *Echtrae Chonnlai*, the people of a 'great *síd*' are called 'the people of Tethra' ([...] *doínib tethrach*; McCone, *Echtrae Chonnlai*, 121–2, paragraphs 5 and 9). McCone's translation 'the people of the sea' is not fully supported by his discussion at 170–71.

[13] Macalister, *Lebor Gabála Érenn*, v, 32.

[14] Ní Shéaghdha, *Tóruigheacht Dhiarmada agus Ghráinne*, 52–3. Although this figure is not explicitly said to belong to the Fomoiri, but rather to be of the 'company' (*muintear*) of the Túatha Dé Donann, the statement of his descent from Ham son of Noah makes the affiliation clear. See the derivation of various leaders of of the Fomoiri from Ham in *Genelach na Fomore* (O'Brien, *Corpus Genealogiarum Hiberniae*, 330–32); also the discussions of attempts made to situate the Fomoiri within the intellectual framework of medieval Christianity in Donahue, 'Grendel and the *Clanna Cain*'; Rodway, 'Mermaids, Leprechauns, and Fomorians'; Clarke, 'The Lore of the Monstrous Races'.

[15] For further brief discussion, see Carey, 'Fomoiri'.

objects of belief. When 'the knowledge of Goibniu' (*fiss Goibnen*) and 'the remedy that Dían Cécht left with his household' (*in slánicid foracab Dian Cecht liamuntir*) are invoked in a ninth-century collection of charms,[16] these allusions to the blacksmith and the physician of the Túatha Dé may refer to figures who, although they were thought to have left behind a legacy of supernatural power, had themselves been relegated to the past. But when another Old Irish charm includes the utterance 'I invoke the three daughters of Flidais' (*Ad·muiniur teōra ingena Flithais*),[17] these women of the Túatha Dé are referred to in the present tense.

In an eleventh-century text which speaks of the legendary queen Mongḟind as a 'female *síd*-dweller' (*bansidaige*), it is said that the night of Samain or Hallowe'en 'is called the feast of Mongḟind by the common folk, for she was powerful and a witch for as long as she was in the body, so that it is therefore that women and the common folk petition her with prayers on the night of Samain'.[18] While the author regards Mongḟind as a witch, accordingly, she is nevertheless described as a *síd*-woman, and is said to be the recipient of prayers from those segments of the population generally excluded from the exercise of authority. At roughly the same period, and again with reference to the festival of Samain, an annal entry for the year 1084 describes a man going to the *síd* of Newgrange every year to receive revelations from Óengus Óc son of the Dagda.[19]

Another suggestive passage is found in *Bethu Phátraic* ('The Life of Patrick'), a composite text of which the greater part is held to date from the late ninth century. This speaks of the saint having left 'guardians' in various parts of Ireland, individuals who had continued living down to the time of writing.[20] Although these 'guardians' are here presented as Christians who had been granted miraculous longevity or immortality, there are clear overlaps between (*a*) this list, (*b*) a list of survivors of the Túatha Dé in the

---

[16] Stokes and Strachan, *Thesaurus Palaeohibernicus*, ii, 248–9.

[17] Kuno Meyer, 'Ein altirischer Heilsegen'.

[18] *[D]ogarar feil Moingḟinde* [...] *icon daescursluagh, ar ba cumachtach si ⁊ bantuathaid cen bai a colaind, conid de cuindgid mna ⁊ daescursluag itcheada aidchi samna fuirri*: Stokes, 'The Death of Crimthann son of Fidach', 178. The date of the text in its surviving form is indicated by a prophecy which seems to refer to the accession of Brian Bóruma (A.D. 1002).

[19] Stokes, 'The Annals of Tigernach', 416. This account is interpreted (not, in my own view, persuasively) as an allegory by Williams, *Ireland's Immortals*, 179–81.

[20] Mulchrone, *Bethu Phátraic*, 75.

saga *Mesca Ulad*, and (*c*) a list of survivors of the Fomoiri in the *mirabilia*-collection *Airne Fíngein*.[21] It appears likely, accordingly, that *Bethu Phátraic* is giving a Christianised reinterpretation of an older belief in immortal beings connected with specific localities. On this hypothesis, it is noteworthy that the list includes one Domangart mac Echach, of whom it is said that:

> his church is Ráith Murbuilc on the side of Slíab Slánga; and a haunch of meat together with its trimmings, and a pitcher of ale, are set before him every Easter, and it is always given to those who celebrate the mass on Easter Monday.
>
> Is sí a chell Ráith Murbuilc hi tóeb Sléibi Sláinge, ⁊ bíid loracc cona timthuc ⁊ chilórnd cormma ara chiunn ar cach Cáisc co tabar do óes oiffrinn díe Lúain Cásc do grés.[22]

Despite the association with Saint Patrick, the location at a church, and its integration in the Easter ritual, this offering of food and drink to a local immortal looks like a reflection of a cult, the antecedents of which are only partly Christian.[23]

While these clues are few and scattered, and in part ambiguous, it should be taken into account that they have been preserved in a Christian literature, produced in an ecclesiastical milieu. If evidence of this kind can be found even here, then there is a strong likelihood that such beliefs were considerably better represented in the oral culture of the laity — the 'women and the common folk' who prayed to Mongḟind. The continuing significance of indigenous supernatural powers among the population at large is, indeed, evident in the extensive body of beliefs concerning the 'fairies': the beings, variously known as 'gentry', *daoine maithe* ('good people'), *bunadh na gcnoc* ('folk of the hills'), and so on, who have been associated with wild places and abandoned habitations down into the twentieth century.[24] And this oral culture

---

[21] Watson, *Mesca Ulad*, 1; Vendryes, *Airne Fíngein*, 14–15. These two passages provide a further example of the occasional interchangeability of Túatha Dé and Fomoiri, noted above.

[22] Mulchrone, *Bethu Phátraic*, 75, ll. 1384–7. More traditions concerning Domangart have been assembled by MacNeill, *The Festival of Lughnasa*, 88–96, 436–7; and Ó Mainnín, *Place-Names of Northern Ireland*, vol. 3, 155–7.

[23] Further discussion in Carey, 'Varieties of Supernatural Contact', 57–8.

[24] Especially striking are instances where a ritual relationship still existed in the last century, as in the case of offerings made to the entity Donn

was part of the background and environment that shaped the authors of the medieval tales, however much or little of it they incorporated in their writings, and however oblique may have been the use that they made of it in doing so.

Despite these various considerations, I shall in what follows be speaking of 'Túatha Dé', not of 'gods' or 'fairies'. While the people of the *síd* may have originated as the former, and may have ended up as the latter, the use of either of these terms would not do justice to the rich and persistent ambiguity which, as we shall see, characterises their nature in the medieval sources.

How do the Túatha Dé figure in narrative? They appear as beings whose dwellings are sometimes said to lie beneath earth or water, or across the sea, but which are usually hidden, and are always mysterious and difficult of access.[25] Although they can be killed, the Túatha Dé appear otherwise to have nothing to fear from age and death;[26] and their beauty and wealth are often mentioned, and are sometimes described at length.[27] They have magical powers: especially powers of transformation or concealment (affecting themselves or others),[28] as well as power over the weather and the heavenly bodies, and over the fruitfulness of the earth.[29] How were such entities to be accounted for in a Christian literature?

It need cause no great surprise that the authors of the tales felt, for the most part, no obligation to provide such explanations: the same is the case for the *fées* of Old French romances, and for

---

Fírinneach: Müller-Lisowski, 'Contributions to a Study in Irish Folklore', 156. For evidence that Donn was in origin an Irish divinity, see Carey, 'Donn, Amairgen, Íth'.

[25] The studies listed on p. ii, n. 1 above can now be supplemented with the examples collected in Carey, 'Ireland, Wales, and Faerie', 144–5.

[26] See the lyrical assertions of unaging immortality in McCone, *Echtrae Chonnlai*, 131–3; Mac Mathúna, *Immram Brain*, 40 §44. Examples of violent death are numerous; besides the many fatalities in *Cath Maige Tuired*, discussed at pp. 34–7 below, there is for instance the carnage inflicted on an Otherworld army by Cú Chulainn in Dillon, *Serglige Con Culainn*, 20–21.

[27] See the examples in 'Ireland, Wales, and Faerie', 145; earlier reflections on the subject in Carey, 'The Waters of Vision and the Gods of Skill', 178–80.

[28] Instances of transformation in O'Rahilly, *Táin Bó Cúailnge*, 30; Bergin and Best, 'Tochmarc Étaíne', 152. For the concealment of the people of the *síde*, see, for example, ibid., 180; and Meyer, 'Macgnimartha Find', 202.

[29] Besides the characterisation of the Dagda in *Tochmarc Étaíne*, cited on p. 10, n. 5 above, see the similar account in *De Gabáil int Ṡída*, discussed at pp. 19–20 below.

elves and other supernatural beings in Norse saga.[30] But because the Túatha Dé were thought to have ruled over Ireland before the coming of the Gaels, they fell within the scheme of Irish legendary history;[31] and because one of the main aims of that scheme was (as noted above) the accommodation of native traditions to the larger framework of Christian sacred history, attempts were made to account for them in historical writing. Here they are sometimes said to have been devils, sometimes humans with magical powers;[32] these rationalisations had patristic authority, and are well attested in references to pagan gods elsewhere in medieval Europe. When the two explanations are first clearly articulated as alternatives by the learned poet Eochaid ua Flainn,[33] some uncertainty is expressed as to which is correct ('the truth concerning them was not known beneath the starry heaven — whether they were of heaven or earth');[34] and the question was still being debated at the end of the Middle Ages. Yet another view, hinted at rather than stated outright, is reflected in some stories from the Old Irish period: that the people of the *síde* were humans, but belonged to a branch of mankind that had somehow escaped the effects of the fall of Adam and Eve.[35]

---

[30] There were however occasional attempts to align the elves, or *álfar*, with less problematical entities. Thus Alaric Hall notes that Snorri Sturluson describes 'light-elves' in terms that appear to be borrowed from an account of angels in the *Elucidarium* of Honorius; and he notes a passage in another work in which they are included among the races of mankind (*Elves in Anglo-Saxon England*, 25–6, 50).

[31] It is however noteworthy that they are absent from the earliest account of Irish legendary history known to us, the listing of the settlements of Ireland that was included, early in the ninth century, in the Cambro-Latin *Historia Brittonum*: Mommsen, 'Historia Brittonum', 154–8 §§13–15. But the Túatha Dé have been added to the Middle Irish version of the same work: van Hamel, *Lebor Bretnach*, 21–2.

[32] Yet another euhemeristic strategy seems to have been the idea that the Túatha Dé were called 'Tribes of Gods' because they regarded their elite as 'gods': their 'people of power' (*áes cumachta*; O'Rahilly, *Táin Bó Cúailnge*, l. 2045) or 'people of skill' (*áes dána*; Carey, 'A *Tuath Dé* Miscellany', 28 §11, 37–9). Williams's phrase 'divinity is aristocracy' (*Ireland's Immortals*, 92) seems like an echo of this conception.

[33] There has been some difference of opinion among scholars as to whether this Eochaid ua Flainn was the same as the scholar Eochaid ua Flannucáin, who died A.D. 1004. The most thorough examination of the question, leading to an answer in the affirmative, is Ó Mainnín, 'Eochaid Ua Flainn'.

[34] *Ni fessa fir fo r[ind]nim / in do nim no do thalmain* (*LL* ll. 1204–5; emended with reference to *for rinnib* in the Book of Fermoy).

[35] For these various interpretive strategies, see Carey, *A Single Ray of the*

The acknowledgement that the Túatha Dé were the gods of the pagan Irish — an identification apparent, as we have seen, in the words of Tírechán — recurs with regard to certain individual figures in *Sanas Cormaic* ('Cormac's Glossary'), a work associated with Cormac mac Cuilennáin, king and bishop of Cashel (died A.D. 908). In a series of passages (all of them, intriguingly, at least partly in Latin), Ana is called 'mother of the Irish gods' (*mater deorum Hibernensium*); Brigit daughter of the Dagda is said to have been regarded as 'goddess [...] of poets' (*deam* [...] *poetarum*) and to have been revered by 'almost all the Irish' (*pene omnes Hibernenses*); and Néit is said to have been 'god of battle for the pagan Gaels' (*dīa catha la geinti Gōideal*). A euhemeristic attitude emerges in the statement that Manannán was a famous merchant who came to be regarded as 'god [...] of the sea' (*deum* [...] *maris*) on account of his skills in navigation and weather prediction; but this matter-of-fact explanation still has as its basis the recognition that this lord among the Túatha Dé had been worshipped as a deity.[36]

When suggestions as to 'who' the Túatha Dé may be are made in the tales, they are often veiled (as in the hints concerning an unfallen race, mentioned above); or else they are external to the story itself. Examples of the latter approach are the colophon at the end of *Serglige Con Culainn*, which explains the whole of the foregoing account of the beauties of the realm of the *síde*, and of the powers of its inhabitants, as a 'ruinous apparition' (*tai[d]bsiu aidmillti*) caused by demons; or the opening of *Echtra Nerai*, which says of the night of Samain, whose magic enables the protagonist to travel between worlds, that 'demons used always to appear on that night' (*doaidbitis demnoie ind oidqi sin dogres*).[37] Nothing else in either tale suggests that the people of the *síde* are demons, any more than there is anything in the account of Cormac mac Airt's visit to the Otherworld hall of Manannán to support that text's concluding assertion that experiences of this kind were encounters with guardian angels.[38] Such explanations in terms of the Christian supernatural may have 'saved the appearances', but they do not look as if they carried imaginative conviction for either author or audience.

Sun, 1–38; further discussion in idem, 'The Old Gods of Ireland'.

[36] Meyer, *Sanas Cormaic*, §§31, 150, 896, 965. Williams, *Ireland's Immortals*, 80–81 notes various possible ambiguities in this evidence; but these considerations do not affect the main point at issue here.

[37] Dillon, *Serglige Con Culainn*, 29; Meyer, 'The Adventures of Nera', 214.

[38] Stokes, 'The Irish Ordeals', 202.

Similarly suggestive is a passage in the tale *Baile in Scáil*, in which his supernatural host identifies himself to Cormac's grandfather Conn Cétchathach:

> The phantom (*scál*) answered them then, and said, 'I am not a phantom nor a spectre, and I have come on account of my fame among you after death. And I am of the race of Adam: my name is Lug son of Eithliu son of Smrith son of Tigernmas (*sic leg.*) [...].
>
> Fri[s-gar]t-sidi dóib íarum ⁊ as-[bert]. 'Nímda-sa scál-sa [⁊ nímda] aurdrach ⁊ is [dom' uirdercus dúib] íar m[bás do-deoch]od ⁊ is de ṡíl Á[daim dom ⁊] is hé mo ṡlonnud, [Lug mac Eth]nen maic Smretha maic Thigernmair [...].[39]

Here there is an abundance of identificatory information; but the various statements appear to cancel one another out. The being whom the author calls a phantom denies that he is a phantom, but then proceeds to say that he has returned from the dead. Having described himself as a human ('of the race of Adam'), he says that he is Lug son of Eithliu, one of the leaders of the Túatha Dé — but then he names his great-grandfather as Tigernmas, not one of the Túatha Dé at all but one of the first generations of the Gaelic settlement. Such a cluster of contradictions can scarcely be inadvertent: both alive and dead, both mortal and divine, Lug does not really belong in any of the categories to which he is assigned, but hovers in what Mark Williams has aptly called a state of 'permanent ontological suspension'.[40]

Although no other European society devoted so much intellectual energy to the question, speculation as to the identity of supernatural 'others' can from time to time be found elsewhere. Thus a twelfth-century Frenchman, Bernardus Silvestris, wrote in his *Cosmographia* of spirits whom he called 'earthly' (*telluros*): dwelling beneath the circle of the moon and watching over the woods, the earth and the waters, with lifespans far greater than our own because their bodies are of 'elemental purity' (*elementali* [...]

---

[39] Murray, *Baile in Scáil*, 34 §7; the text of Oxford, Bodleian Library, Rawlinson MS B 512, supplemented from London, BL Harley MS 5280 where it is illegible.

[40] *Ireland's Immortals*, 492. Subsequently he says of the Túatha Dé collectively that 'like Lug in "The Phantom's Frenzy", they are their own ghosts' (p. 495).

puritate).[41] His younger contemporary Gervase of Tilbury, having described what appeared to be physical beings dwelling 'in caves and the banks of rivers' (*in cauernis et ripis fluminum*), who stole human children and took men as lovers, suggested that they were spirits who had assumed bodies of air.[42] But explanations of this sort, even when they invoked the Fathers of the Church, matched the 'others' themselves only imperfectly, and always had a rather provisional character. As C.S. Lewis said of the place of such beings in medieval European thought more generally: 'No agreement was achieved. As long as the Fairies remained at all they remained evasive'.[43]

---

[41] Bernardus Silvestris, *Cosmographia*, 136.

[42] Gervase of Tilbury, *Otia Imperialia*, 716–31. Throughout most of his discussion, Gervase calls male and female beings of this sort *draci* and *lamiae* respectively; but he also refers to the latter as *fadae*, i.e. *fées* or fairies.

[43] *The Discarded Image*, 138. As one of this book's anonymous readers has pointed out to me, an interesting contrast is afforded by the treatment of the supernatural entities called *jinn* in Islam. Not only is their existence as a distinct class of being prominently affirmed, as when God states in *Qur'ān* 51:56–7 that he has created *jinn* as well as humans in order that they should worship him; but it is even said that some of the *jinn* accepted the true religion, and preached it to their fellows (46:29–31, 72:1–15).

3. Tales Related to *Táin Bó Cúailnge*

In the following chapters, an attempt will be made to survey the tales that can most reasonably be held to belong to a 'mythological cycle'. As we have already seen, the very concept of such a cycle is problematical, and further complications will come to light as we proceed. As a label, however, the term is useful at least insofar as it directs our attention to a remarkable collection of material, and prompts us to recognise how far we have still to go in our efforts to understand it.

The first stories to be considered, all of them dating from the Old Irish period, have more in common than a concern with the Túatha Dé and the *síde*: all of them also have some connection, direct or indirect, with the background of the legendary conflict that forms the subject of the central narrative of the Ulster cycle, the great tale *Táin Bó Cúailnge*.

The short tale ***De Gabáil int Ṡída*** ('Concerning the Taking of the *Síd*'; *CLH* §1036) was assigned by Thurneysen to the ninth century at latest;[1] I can see no reason why it could not be as early as the eighth. It survives in two manuscripts, the Book of Leinster and RIA MS D.iv.2 (catalogue number 1223): in the former the language is still essentially Old Irish, while in the latter it has been much modernised.

The central figure is the Dagda (here also called Dagán), king of the Túatha Dé or Fir Dé, the magnitude of whose power is illustrated by various of his deeds. After the sons of Míl (i.e., the leaders of the Gaelic settlement) had conquered Ireland, the Dagda was able to compel them to make a treaty (*cairddes*) with him by causing their grain and milk to be destroyed until they capitulated: this is interesting as testimony to the persistence, even in literature produced by ecclesiastical authors, of the idea that human subsistence depended on a good relationship with the native supernatural. The Dagda is also celebrated for having allocated the *síde* among the various Fir Dé at the beginning of his reign. There follows an account of how the Dagda's son, the Mac Óc, obtained his father's own dwelling from him by a trick, asking for it only

[1] *Die irische Helden- und Königsage*, 604; he was followed in this estimate by Hull, '*De Gabáil in t-Ṡída*', 54. Hull's edition, based on the two surviving copies, is to be consulted. The most recent detailed examination of this brief text to be published, including his own edition and translation, is that of Bondarenko, *Studies in Irish Mythology*, 37–40. The tale has also been edited by Maher, 'De Gabáil int Ṡída'.

for 'a day and a night', but then asserting that 'the whole world is day and night': thus he became the master of Síd in Broga, the mound of Newgrange. Other versions of this seizure of Síd in Broga are related in *Tochmarc Étaíne* and in *Altram Tighe Dá Mheadar* (discussed below). In a concluding paragraph, found only in the Book of Leinster, the supernatural abundance of this Otherworld realm is described.[2]

In both manuscripts, the text immediately follows a list of the *remscéla* ('fore-tales') of *Táin Bó Cúailnge*, at or near the head of which its title is included:[3] this, presumably, is the reason for its preservation. In fact, however, the story has no direct connection with the events of the *Táin*: Norbert Backhaus has argued that it is really given as a 'fore-tale' of *Aislinge Óenguso*, which is also listed here as one of the *Táin*'s *remscéla*.[4]

Aislinge Óenguso ('The Dream of Óengus'; *CLH* §986) survives only in a single vellum manuscript, London, BL Egerton MS 1782,[5] where it too forms part of an extended series of *remscéla* to the *Táin*. Thurneysen at first considered it to be 'not very old', suggesting that it was written in the ninth or tenth century;[6] but he was subsequently persuaded by the arguments of the text's editor, Francis Shaw, for a date of composition in the eighth.[7] Knowledge

---

[2] Thurneysen at first considered this final passage to be 'in jüngerer Sprache' (*Die irische Helden- und Königsage*, 605), but according to Hull he later came to regard it as being 'linguistically as old as the remainder' ('*De Gabáil in t-Ṡída*', 54 n. 1).

[3] Thurneysen, *Die irische Helden- und Königsage*, 248–51.

[4] 'The Structure of the List of *Remscéla Tána Bó Cualngi*', 21 n. 11. Tom Chadwin similarly characterises it as what he calls a '*remremscél*': 'merely a *remscél* to *Aislinge Óenguso* rather than to *TBC* itself'; moreover, 'it has no causal relationship with *Aislinge Óenguso*, but merely provides general information relating to the opening of it' ('The *Remscéla Tána Bó Cualngi*', 73–4). In the Book of Leinster list, *Aislinge Óenguso* in fact immediately follows *De Gabáil int Ṡída*. For a sceptical review of Chadwin's assessment, see now Maher, '*De Gabáil int Ṡída: Remscél* or *Remremscél*?'.

[5] It is also found in paper transcripts of the same manuscript: to those listed by Shaw, *The Dream of Óengus*, 29 n. 1, can be added (as Kevin Murray points out to me) Longford, St Mel's College MS 9. The preservation of such tales in the modern scribal tradition is important evidence of their continuing importance. Where late manuscripts merely provide copies of earlier and still surviving witnesses, however, they will not be further noted here.

[6] *Die irische Helden- und Königsage*, 301.

[7] Shaw, *The Dream of Óengus*, 32–8. Shaw noted the difficulties in interpreting the evidence, characterising the tale's language as 'Old Irish, with a

of the story is reflected in the brief eschatological tract 'The Lore of the Fiery Arrow', preserved in An Leabhar Breac (RIA MS 23.P.16; catalogue number 1230) and in RIA MS D.iv.2.[8]

The Mac Óc, here referred to by his other name Óengus, falls into a decline on account of his love for a girl who appears to him in his sleep. After the cause of his debility has been discovered by the physician of Conchobur mac Nesa, king of the Ulaid, a search for the maiden is instituted: first by Óengus's mother Boand, then by his father the Dagda (here called 'king of the *síde* of Ireland'), and finally by Bodb ('king of the *síde* of Munster'). She is finally found, with a multitude of companions, beside a lake in Tipperary: her name is Cáer Ibormeith, and she comes from a *síd* in Connacht.

The Dagda appeals for help to Ailill and Medb, the rulers of Connacht. They storm the *síd* which is her home and capture her father, but he claims to have no power over her. In the end Óengus is only able to obtain her love when she and the other maidens appear on the lake in the shape of swans: he transforms himself also into a swan in order to embrace her, and then takes her back to his dwelling in Bruig na Bóinne (the territory dominated by Síd in Broga). This, we are told, was the reason for Óengus's alliance with Ailill and Medb, and hence for his joining them when they went to seize the bull of Cúailnge.

Such an alliance with Óengus is not mentioned in the *Táin* itself; and this tangential association was accordingly viewed with suspicion by Shaw. He stated that

> there is grave reason to believe that the connection of our story with the great epic is fictitious and purely artificial [...]. If this were so we should have to assume that the last paragraph of the text, the paragraph in which the link with the Táin is forged, is a later addition to the text.[9]

Subsequently, however, Hugh Fogarty has proposed that, although the story originated independently of the *Táin*, its positioning as a *remscél* reflects recognition of significant thematic correspondences between the two narratives.[10] Other recent studies of the tale

very strong leaven of early and late Middle Irish forms'. See now Meid, *Die Suche nach der Traumfrau*, 48–9.

[8] Carey et al. (eds), *The End and Beyond*, 705–13.

[9] Shaw, *The Dream of Óengus*, 25.

[10] '*Aislinge Óenguso*'. So far as I am aware, none of those who have discussed the question of the story's relationship to the *Táin* have mentioned the

are that of Tomás Ó Cathasaigh, who traces the growth of knowledge throughout the narrative, and compares it with the *Táin* on the basis that each can be described as involving 'the crucial role of allies in the achievement of ends';[11] and that of Brenda Gray, for whom it is 'an eschatological, Christian-Platonic parable on the spiritual journey of the soul, and an erotic allegory on divine love', the most telling parallels to which are to be found in Plato's dialogues themselves.[12]

De Chophur in Dá Muccida ('Concerning the Contention/Conception (?) of the Two Swineherds'; *CLH* §1035) is also included in the collections of *remscéla* in the Book of Leinster and in Egerton MS 1782.[13] Thurneysen held that the Book of Leinster preserves something close to the original text, which he tentatively dated to the ninth century; while the Egerton version has been expanded with several additions from other *remscéla* (including *Aislinge Óenguso*), and can be assigned to the first half of the twelfth century.[14] An allusion to Mongán mac Fíachnai as one who could transform himself 'into every shape' suggests familiarity with Manannán's prophecy of Mongán in *Immram Brain* ('The Voyage of Bran').[15]

Ochall, king of the *síde* of Connacht, and Bodb, king of the *síde* of Munster, each had a swineherd. The two were friends, and

---

allusion, in the Middle Irish poem *Dúan in Chethrachat Cest*, to a story in which Óengus is said to have slain many warriors of the Ulaid and to have overcome their greatest heroes (see pp. 41–2, n. 18 below). Here we do in fact find him acting as the antagonist of the enemies of Medb and Ailill.

[11] 'Knowledge and Power in *Aislinge Óenguso*'.

[12] 'Reading *Aislinge Óenguso*'. The lack of any evidence that these dialogues were known in Ireland, or indeed in western Europe, at the time of *Aislinge Óenguso*'s composition is of course an argument against any direct influence. With a more plausible range of comparanda, but also very speculatively, Mark Williams suggests that Óengus's lovesickness might have been interpreted as 'an allegory of poetic composition' (*Ireland's Immortals*, 177); he states that he hopes to pursue his analysis of this tale in a future publication.

[13] There is a collection of glosses drawn from the Book of Leinster version of the tale in TCD MS 1337 (shelf-mark H 3.18; Roider, *De Chophur in Da Muccida*, 60–61); and the late Ulster saga *Cath Findchorad* borrows the description of the bulls, in what the editor describes as a 'fuller and less corrupt version' than that in the Book of Leinster (Dobbs, 'The Battle of Findchorad', 397, 400–403).

[14] *Die irische Helden- und Königsage*, 277–8; echoed by Roider, *De Chophur in Da Muccida*, 19.

[15] Mac Mathúna, *Immram Brain*, 42, 55 §53.

were also powerful magicians, with the ability to assume all shapes. Eventually they fell out in a dispute over which of them had the greater power. They fought one another as crows (or hawks?), as water-monsters, as stags, as champions (*fénnidi*), as spectres, and as dragons. They then became two worms and dropped into two pools: one was swallowed by a cow in Ulster, and the other by a cow in Connacht. These cows subsequently gave birth to the two bulls that would give rise to the great war of the *Táin*.

It is noteworthy that this story, like *Aislinge Óenguso*, concerns itself with the *síde* of Munster and Connacht; apart from a stray allusion in *Togail Bruidne Da Derga*, moreover, these appear to be the only Old Irish texts to mention Bodb.[16] It may therefore not be unreasonable to suppose that the two tales could derive from a common background.[17] We have already noted that there appears also to be some relationship between *Aislinge Óenguso* and *De Gabáil int Ṡída*: in this connection, it may be significant that the latter opens with an account of a treaty (*cairddes*) guaranteeing the fruitfulness of crops and flocks, while the friendship (*cairddes*) of the two swineherds is said to have soured because they used their powers to prevent one another's swine from feeding properly.[18]

The edition by Ulrike Roider gives particular attention to the possibility that the transformations of the swineherds reflect earlier Celtic ideas concerning the wanderings of the soul, a hypothesis for which she offers as tentative support an argument that the mysterious word *cophur* in the title might be cognate with the Sanskrit *saṃsāra*, and could accordingly be translated as 'cyclical rebirth'.[19] This proposal has elicited a rebuttal from Christoph Dröge, who argues that the Sanskrit term only came to be associated with reincarnation relatively late in its semantic

[16] Knott, *Togail Bruidne Da Derga*, l. 1393. Here again, intriguingly, the context is the mention of a 'swineherd of Bodb from Síd ar Ḟemun' (*muccaid Boidb a Síd ar Ḟemin*); but he is named Nár, rather than Friuch as in the present tale. *Bodb Síde Femin* is also mentioned in *Airne Fíngein* (ed. Vendryes, 15), a text belonging either to the late Old Irish or the early Middle Irish period.

[17] A suggested relationship of a different kind was noted by Carney, who opined that 'a case could be made for the common authorship of *T[áin] B[ó] F[r]aích* and *Aislinge Oengussa*' (*Studies in Irish Literature and History*, 65).

[18] On the connotations of *cairddes* in *Aislinge Óenguso* in particular, see Fogarty, '*Aislinge Óenguso*'.

[19] *De Chophur in Da Muccida*, 62–78.

development.[20] The question has been revisited by Grigory Bondarenko, who associates the transformations of the swineherds with 'the migration of the soul in Celtic myth', but stresses that these marvels are here portrayed from a Christian, and hence critical, perspective.[21]

A further interesting analogue in Welsh tradition has not yet (to my knowledge) been considered in this connection. The Middle Welsh tale *Cyfranc Lludd a Lleuelys* ('The Story of Lludd and Lleuelys') speaks of two dragons (one native and one foreign) that fight every year, one of them uttering a cry that blights the fertility of the land and its inhabitants. This situation is brought to an end when Lludd king of Britain arranges that, when the dragons after their combat are transformed into piglets (*parchell*) and descend to the ground, they shall sink into a vessel of mead and fall asleep, after which they can be confined in the stronghold of Dinas Emrys, in the mountains of Eryri in northern Wales.[22] This episode retrospectively supplies the background for a story in a much older text, *Historia Brittonum* (early ninth century), in which two dragons or worms (*uermes*) are found buried beneath the foundations of the stronghold which is eventually named Dinas Emrys: the dragons represent the Britons and the English, and the course of their conflict foretokens the struggles of those two peoples.[23] The presence in both the Irish and the Welsh tales of battle between shape-shifting theriomorphic antagonists, their sinking into liquid at the conclusion of their combat, and the link between their hostilities and the military destinies of two enemy peoples; together with the analogy between famished animals in one story and blighted crops in the other, render it difficult to believe that there is not some connection between them. But further investigation will be needed before any more can be made of this attractive possibility.

Given that three important stories concerning the people of the *síde* are also *remscéla* to the *Táin*, it seems appropriate that ***Echtra Nerai*** ('The Adventure of Nera'; *CLH* §1050) should be mentioned at this point as well.[24] Although the tale's protagonist is

---

[20] 'Ein irischer *saṃsāra*?', 261–8.

[21] *Studies in Irish Mythology*, 183–95.

[22] Roberts, *Cyfranc Lludd a Llefelys*, 2, 4–5.

[23] Mommsen, 'Historia Brittonum', 183–6.

[24] Admittedly, this transgresses a principle which I articulated earlier, and opens the way for considering further tales which I will however not be discussing. One candidate, as Kevin Murray points out to me, would be the

a mortal, the narrative is largely concerned with adventures in the *síd* of Crúachan; and these adventures, like those of the swineherds, are portrayed as being the ultimate cause of the cattle-raid of Cúailnge. The text appears (immediately preceding *De Chophur in Dá Muccida*) as one of the *remscéla* in Egerton MS 1782, and also (with the title *Tain Bé Aingen*) in a small gathering of *remscéla* which follows the copy of the *Táin* in the Yellow Book of Lecan (TCD MS 1318; shelf-mark H 2.16); there is also a fragment of the story in Liber Flavus Fergusiorum (RIA MS 23.O.48; catalogue number 476).[25] Thurneysen at first placed its composition 'hardly earlier than the tenth century', but subsequently found 'no serious obstacle' to a date in the eighth.[26]

No brief synopsis can do justice to the complexities of the story's plot.[27] Nera, a man belonging to the household of Ailill and Medb, ventures abroad on the night of Samain and is obliged to become a servant of the ruler of the *síd* of Crúachan. He learns that the inhabitants of the *síd* are planning a raid on the royal

---

brief narrative edited by Vernam Hull under the title *Ces Ulad*, describing Cú Chulainn's dealings with the *síd*-folk Elcmaire and Feidelm. The only copy is included in a series of miscellaneous short pieces in Harley MS 5280, a few pages before the anecdotes *Togail Síde Truim* and *Bruigen Séinbic hIdbric* (see below). Due to the corrupt nature of the text, Hull did not feel able to propose any dating more definite than 'before the middle of the twelfth century'; he suspected, however, that the original composition of *Ces Ulad* might go back to the Old Irish period ('Ces Ulad', 307–9).

[25] Meyer, 'The Adventures of Nera'. The fragment in Liber Flavus Fergusiorum, omitted from Thurneysen's discussion of the story and not used in Meyer's edition, is published in Carey, 'Sequence and Causation', 73–4. Thurneysen's tentative revised judgement, communicated to Ó Duilearga in a letter dated 28 November 1938, was based on the form *blednai* (for standard *blíadnai*), at l. 142 of Meyer's edition. Both Ó Coileáin ('*Echtrae Nerai* and its Analogues', 428) and Toner ('Narrative, Death and the Otherworld', 107) have regarded this evidence with scepticism; but their own counter-arguments do not seem to me to be compelling. The question of whether the text was first composed early or late in the Old Irish period appears still to be an open one.

[26] *Die irische Helden- und Königsage*, 312; Ó Duilearga, 'Nera and the Dead Man', 522 n. 5.

[27] For an attempt to come to grips with some of the more recalcitrant of these, see Carey, 'Sequence and Causation'. As in the case of *Tochmarc Becfola* (see below), I have argued that anomalies in the logic of the narrative reflect the author's attempt to depict Otherworld time, rather than (as Thurneysen held) the inept conflation of discrepant versions on the part of a redactor. The same conclusion has been reached on other grounds by Ó Flaithearta, '*Echtra Nerai*', 172–4; and by Toner, 'Narrative, Death and the Otherworld', 116–20.

stronghold; then, helped by the *síd*-woman who has become his consort, he manages to return and warn his people so that they can make a preemptive attack of their own. Meanwhile the woman has born him a son, and given the child a cow. This cow is stolen by the war-goddess known as the Morrígain, and is taken to Ulster where it is impregnated by the Donn, the bull of Cúailnge; as she is taking the cow back to Connacht, the Morrígain is challenged by Cú Chulainn.[28] After the assault on the *síd*, the calf which the cow has by now born fights against the Findbennach, the great bull of Connacht, and Medb swears that she will not rest until she has brought about a combat between the Findbennach and the calf's sire. This, then, is the reason for the expedition to seize the Donn Cúailnge.

The first close investigation of the story was concerned only with its beginning: here Nera, responding to a challenge from Ailill to go out into the night and bind the corpse of a hanged man, is obliged to take the uncannily animated corpse onto his back, and to visit three houses with varying results. The folklorist Séamus Ó Duilearga noted the unmistakable resemblance of this scene to a folktale recorded throughout the Gaeltachtaí in modern times, going so far as to say that it is 'quite evident that [this episode of] Echtra Nerai and the modern folktale are identical', and to speak of the former as 'one of the oldest Irish folk-tales which has come down to us'.[29]

By contrast with Ó Duilearga's approach, Alden Watson has taken the unity of the story as a given, subjecting it to a structuralist analysis drawing on the methods of Claude Lévi-Strauss: in his view '*Echtra Nerai* is a tale whose primary concern is an elucidation of sovereignty in relation to the function of the hero'.[30] While some of Watson's arguments have been regarded as 'unconvincing',[31] subsequent scholars have agreed with him in detecting a concern with sovereignty in the tale. Thus Leonie Duignan, who sees sovereignty as being a fundamental theme in

[28] A more extended account of this episode provides the basis of the *remscél* entitled *Táin Bó Regamna*: the standard edition is Corthals, *Táin Bó Regamna*. The relationship between the two stories, and that of both with *Táin Bó Cúailnge*, have been examined by Ó Flaithearta, '*Echtra Nerai*'.

[29] 'Nera and the Dead Man', 532, 522. His view that this episode has nothing to do with the rest of the tale (ibid., 522) has been challenged by Ó Coileáin, '*Echtrae Nerai* and its Analogues', who notes further resemblances with the Irish folktale known as 'The fairy hill is on fire!'.

[30] Watson, 'A Structural Analysis', 142.

[31] Ó Coileáin, '*Echtra Nerai* and its Analogues', 440.

all *echtrai*, considers *Echtra Nerai* to be no exception in this regard even though Nera's own lack of royal status is unusual;[32] while Gregory Toner, who has shed important new light on the narrative by pointing out that Nera is not a warrior but rather a steward or *rechtaire*, demonstrates the centrality of kingship in the text even as he notes weaknesses in Watson's analysis.[33] There can indeed be little doubt of this centrality, given the crucial importance attributed to the seizure from the *síd* by the men of Connacht of the 'crown of Brión' (*barr Briúin*): a treasure clearly connected with the Uí Briúin dynasty, who held the provincial kingship of Connacht at the time of the story's composition.[34]

Although, as will be seen in the next chapter, further tales concerning the realm of the *síde* and its inhabitants were composed in the Old Irish period, it is striking that so many are to varying degrees associated with the antecedents of the war of the Donn Cúailnge. Something similar seems to be present in *Tochmarc Étaíne* (discussed below), where a struggle between a king of Ireland and one of the lords of the *síde* sows the seeds of a catastrophic slaughter with repercussions for the sovereignty of all Ireland;[35] and in *Cath Maige Mucrama*, where the anger of the people of the *síde* is responsible for another disastrous battle with far-reaching consequences.[36] The underlying idea may be that

---

[32] *The Echtrae*, 156–7.

[33] 'Narrative, Death and the Otherworld', 111–14.

[34] A point also made by Toner, ibid., 116. I do not however agree with him that the crown was originally the property of the mortal kings of Connacht and had been taken from them by the people of the *síd*, so that its seizure at the end of the tale was in fact its recovery. Brión, with whom the crown is associated, was held to have lived several centuries *after* the reign of Ailill and Medb, so that I can see no grounds for thinking that the crown did not originate in the *síd*. When it is described as the 'diadem of gold that is wont to be on the head of the king' (*mionn n-oir bis for cionn ind rig*; Meyer, 'The Adventures of Nera', l. 71), it is evidently conceived to be at that point a token of the kingship of the *síd*, not of the kingship of Connacht.

[35] This connection is made explicit in the short version of *Togail Bruidne Da Derga*, attributed to the lost manuscript Cín Dromma Snechtai: 'It is the people of the *síd* of Brí Léith who arranged that destruction, because their *síd* was dug up when Eochaid was seeking Étain' (*is áes síde Breg Leith dorinólsat in n-orgain fo bíth tonaidbecht forro a síd oc cuinchid Étaíne le Echdaig*; *LU* ll. 8014–16).

[36] O Daly, *Cath Maige Mucrama*: Lugaid Mac Con, who will eventually bring about the deaths of the kings of Ireland and Munster, is turned against them in a quarrel engineered as an act of revenge by the people of a *síd*.

events of the greatest magnitude require a supernatural cause: thus in Greek mythology the Trojan War was explained as being due to a quarrel between goddesses on Olympus, or indeed to the will of Zeus.[37]

Further discussion in Ó Cathasaigh, 'The Theme of Lommrad'.

[37] The celebrated story of the judgement of Paris is briefly alluded to by Homer, *Iliad* xxiv, 27–30. According to a summary in the *Chrestomathy* of Proclus, the episode was related in the lost epic *Cypria*; and one surviving fragment of that poem portrays the war as having been deliberately brought about by Zeus himself, in order to reduce the world's excessive population (Evelyn-White, *Hesiod; the Homeric Hymns and Homerica*, 488–9, 496–7).

4. Further Old Irish Tales

Although references and borrowings elsewhere in the literature indicate that the story ***Tochmarc Étaíne*** ('The Wooing of Étaín'; *CLH* §1114) was widely known, only one complete copy has survived: this is in the Yellow Book of Lecan. There is a second copy, which has however suffered the loss of several leaves, in Lebor na hUidre (RIA MS 23.E.25; catalogue number 1229). Thurneysen considered that *Tochmarc Étaíne* 'can, on the basis of language, be assigned to the ninth century, but its reworking belongs approximately to the second half of the eleventh': this view has been accepted by subsequent scholars.[1] The story has often been translated, paraphrased and summarised. In the synopsis that follows, I shall pay most attention to those elements which concern the realm of the *síde*.

Tochmarc Étaíne consists in fact of three stories, bound together by a single title and by a continuing line of narrative. The first of these begins with an account of the conception of the Mac Óc as the result of an affair between the Dagda and Boand, and goes on to relate how he came to possess the *síd* of Bruig na Bóinne (a version of the tale given in *De Gabáil int Ṡída*).[2] He then won the beautiful Étaín as a wife for his fosterfather Midir, altering the landscape of Ulster in the process. But Midir already had a wife, the formidable Fúamnach, who was both jealous and skilled in magic. Fúamnach enchanted Étaín so that she became a fly. After many adventures, the transformed Étaín fell into a vessel of wine and was swallowed by a woman who then conceived and gave birth to her as a mortal child. One thousand and twelve years had passed since her first begetting. Étaín grew up with no memory of her former existence, and when on one occasion Midir appeared to her it does not seem that she recognised him. The Mac Óc tracked Fúamnach down and killed her.

The second part tells how Étaín became the wife of Eochaid Airem, king of Ireland: that Eochaid's marriage to her is indispensable to his full exercise of his kingship is one of the indications in the tale that Étaín belongs to the category of female

[1] *Die irische Helden- und Königsage*, 598; Bergin and Best, 'Tochmarc Étaíne', 139; Dillon, *Early Irish Literature*, 54.

[2] Another version of these events, differing from that in *Tochmarc Étaíne* in several significant details, is given in the poem *Sect.o.f.n.* Edition and translation in Gwynn, 'Cináed úa hArtacáin's Poem'; with recent discussion in Theuerkauf, 'A Note on *Sect.o.f.n.*'.

figures (often supernatural) who function in Irish legend as personifications of sovereignty.[3] Eochaid's brother Ailill fell ill for love of her, and Étaín agreed to sleep with him so that he could regain his health. Instead of Ailill, however, a stranger came to the tryst. He eventually identified himself as Midir, explained that he had caused Ailill's infatuation, and asked Étaín to go away with him. She declined to do so without her husband's leave. Midir departed, and Ailill recovered from his sickness.

In the third part, Midir induced Eochaid (who did not know his identity) to play the board game *fidchell* with him several times. At first Eochaid won, and was able to make a series of demands of Midir (including the advantageous reshaping of parts of the landscape). But Midir won the last game, and insisted on being allowed to embrace and kiss Étaín. Despite Eochaid's attempts to obstruct him, Midir was able to come and claim this prize, and he made use of the opportunity to transform himself and Étaín into swans and to fly away with her. First by brute force, and then with the aid of magic, Eochaid set about digging up Síd Ban Find in Munster, and subsequently Midir's own *síd* of Brí Léith. At length Midir said that he would give Étaín back to him; but Eochaid must choose her out of a group of fifty women who all looked exactly like her. Eochaid made his choice, only to be later informed by Midir that he had selected his own daughter.[4] When she gave birth to a girl, Eochaid ordered that this child of incest be exposed; but she was reared by a herdsman and his wife, and grew up to become the mother of Conaire Már, one of the greatest of the legendary kings of Ireland. Eochaid subsequently came to a violent end, of which various accounts are given.

The second part of the story also appears as an autonomous tale elsewhere in the Yellow Book of Lecan.[5] Moreover, what Lucius Gwynn has described as a 'turgid re-telling' of this episode, supplemented with a scene from *Togail Bruidne Da Derga* (describing Eochaid's first meeting with Étaín) and a version of the *dindṡenchas* of Ráith Chrúachna (which gives an alternative account of how Midir carried off Étaín, together with one of her handmaids), provides the beginning of a compilatory narrative in Egerton MS 1782.[6] Gwynn proposed for this compilation a date in

[3] Discussion, for example, in Ó Cathasaigh, '*Tochmarc Étaíne* II', 130–33.

[4] For the possibility that a further animal metamorphosis may be present at this point in the story, see Carey, 'The Final Transformation of Étaín'.

[5] Bergin and Best, 'Tochmarc Étaíne', 162–73.

[6] The second half of this work is a late recension of *Togail Bruidne Da Derga*

the twelfth or thirteenth century.[7]

Myles Dillon surely spoke for many when he wrote of the earlier version of the tale that it has 'a strange beauty [...] which perhaps no other Irish story shares'.[8] *Tochmarc Étaíne* has often been regarded, especially in its first section, as a particularly close reflection of pre-Christian Irish myth, despite its composition by a medieval Christian author. Even if a 'mythological' flavour be acknowledged, however, this can be variously interpreted, as when Mark Williams suggests that the portrayal of the Dagda may have been modelled on literary accounts of the Roman god Jupiter, perhaps specifically on references to him in the writings of Isidore of Seville.[9] And Thomas Charles-Edwards has shown that the actions of the Túatha Dé in the story, whatever other resonances they may have, can be understood in terms of the legal usage and dynastic geography of the eighth and ninth centuries.[10] But for all that, this is a tale which has the relationship between the supernatural and the mortal realms as a central concern, and this is reflected in many of its themes: examples are Étaín's metamorphoses and rebirth; the evocation of the qualities of a beatific Otherworld;[11] the transgression of the categories of time and space;[12] and the difficulties confronted, and strategies adopted, in order to force entry into a *síd*.[13]

The stories discussed so far — *De Gabáil int Ṡída*, *Aislinge Óenguso*, *De Chophur in Dá Muccida*, *Echtra Nerai* and *Tochmarc Étaíne*

---

as a whole.

[7] Gwynn, 'The Two Versions of Tochmarc Étaíne'; Gwynn, 'The Recensions of the Saga "Togail Bruidne Da Derga"', 212–17; Thurneysen, *Die irische Helden- und Königsage*, 657–63.

[8] *Irish Sagas*, 17.

[9] *Ireland's Immortals*, 87. Cf. Charles-Edwards's remark concerning the Dagda's adultery with Boand: 'If the author or his contemporary readers had read Augustine's *City of God*, Book VII, they would have known that this was the kind of thing that pagan gods get up to all the time' ('*Tochmarc Étaíne*', 166 n. 10).

[10] Ibid.

[11] The principal testimony in this regard is afforded by Midir's poetic address to Étaín: Bergin and Best, 'Tochmarc Étaíne', 180–83.

[12] Besides the Dagda's lengthening of a single day (ibid., 143–4), I argue in 'Identity, Time and the Otherworld' that dilation of time within the *síd* must be assumed to account for the sexual maturity of Eochaid's daughter at the end of the tale. In the poem referred to in the preceding note, a 'great land' (*tír már*) lies within, or is reached via, the hollow hill of Brí Léith.

[13] Bergin and Best, 'Tochmarc Étaíne', 184–5.

— comprise the greater part of the Old Irish texts that can be reasonably assigned to a notional 'mythological cycle'. While the viability of this category is, as we have seen, open to serious doubt, it is striking that these tales can be seen to be interrelated in other ways. All of them set the stage for the great events of Irish epic: *Aislinge Óenguso*, *De Chophur in Dá Muccida* and *Echtra Nerai* for the great war narrated in *Táin Bó Cúailnge*; *Tochmarc Étaíne* for the life and downfall of Conaire Már as told in *Togail Bruidne Da Derga*; *De Gabáil int Ṡída* for the unfolding of *Tochmarc Étaíne* itself.

As we have seen, other elements connect these tales as well. The figures of the Dagda and his son are prominent in *De Gabáil int Ṡída*, *Aislinge Óenguso* and *Tochmarc Étaíne*; Bodb figures in *Aislinge Óenguso* and *De Chophur in Dá Muccida*; and the king of the *síde* of Connacht is a character in *De Chophur in Dá Muccida* and *Echtra Nerai*. A formal alliance called a *cairddes* plays a crucial role in *De Gabáil int Ṡída*, in *Aislinge Óenguso*, and in *De Chophur in Dá Muccida*. However the circumstance is to be understood, these stories of the people of the *síde* constitute a distinct group. This group's distinctness is thrown into further relief by the fact that two more Old Irish tales, although also concerned with 'Otherworld' folk and/or the Túatha Dé, exhibit none of these characteristics: these are *Tochmarc Becḟola* and *Cath Maige Tuired*.

Tochmarc Becḟola ('The Wooing of Becḟola'; *CLH* §1112) is not generally included in the 'mythological cycle'; but, as an account of the supernatural adventures of a figure who evidently belongs to the people of the *síde*, it merits consideration here. It exists in two recensions: one, preserved in the Yellow Book of Lecan and in TCD MS 1337, has been said by Myles Dillon to be 'not later than the ninth century', while Máire Bhreathnach tentatively dates 'the original composition to the late ninth or early tenth century'.[14] The second recension, in London, BL Egerton MS 1781 and RIA MS B.iv.1 (catalogue number 236), is placed by Bhreathnach 'towards the end of the twelfth century, perhaps later'.[15]

We are told how Díarmait mac Áedo Sláine, a king of Tara whose death is placed by the annals in the year 664 or 667, met a beautiful woman who was travelling by herself in a chariot. He

---

[14] Dillon, 'The Wooing of Becfhola', 11; Bhreathnach, 'A New Edition of Tochmarc Becfhola', 68–70.

[15] Ibid., 71.

took her back to Tara to be his consort: since he had given her no bride-price apart from a brooch, she came to be called Becḟola (as if from *becc* 'small' and *folud* 'property'). She fell in love with Díarmait's fosterson, and prevailed upon him to elope with her. In the event, however, he did not come to their tryst: after losing the handmaid who had accompanied her she wandered in the forest, coming at length to the campfire of a mysterious warrior. The stranger brought her to a magnificent but apparently empty hall on an island, where they were magically provided with food; next morning, he and his three brothers fought with their four cousins for possession of the island. Becḟola offered herself to the stranger, but he declined to take her until he had won his inheritance. She returned to Tara to find that no time had elapsed during her absence. In a year's time, the warrior came to Tara to say that another battle for the island had been fought, a conflict of which he was the sole survivor. Becḟola went away with him, and as she departed was denounced by Díarmait as an evil spirit (*urchód*). It was subsequently revealed that the magical island was Devenish, site of an ecclesiastical settlement in County Fermanagh, and Díarmait made a gift to the monastery there of the treasure found on the bodies of the seven slain warriors.

This story has been compared with the Tristan legend and its various analogues,[16] but resemblances to the second part of *Tochmarc Étaíne* seem at least as likely to be significant, and do not appear to have attracted comment hitherto. Like Étaín in *Togail Bruidne Da Derga*,[17] Becḟola is alone when first encountered by the king of Tara who later makes her his wife, and in both cases the scene provides the occasion for an extended description of the heroine's appearance. Becḟola, like Étaín, is evidently of supernatural origin, and finally disappears into the Otherworld; but in the main narrative she appears to be unaware that she is not like other mortals. Like Étaín, she makes an assignation with a man closely related to her husband (brother in one case, fosterson in the other), but the prospective lover fails to appear at the designated place. Instead, she meets a splendid supernatural warrior, who eventually carries her off. It is striking that all of these elements can be paralleled specifically in the version of the Étaín story which forms the first part of the compilation in Egerton MS 1782; even Becḟola's departure from

[16] Thus Carney, *Studies in Irish Literature and History*, 229–30; cf. Bhreathnach, 'A New Edition', 64–6.
[17] Knott, *Togail Bruidne Da Derga*, 1–2.

Tara accompanied by a handmaid can be compared with the episode borrowed from the *dindṡenchas* of Ráith Chrúachna.

Becḟola's Otherworld experiences involve anomalies of mortal whereabouts and duration: the supernatural island at the heart of the story seems sometimes to be in Leinster and sometimes in Connacht, and the entirety of her adventure takes no time at all from the perspective of those who have stayed in Tara. These oddities led James Carney, memorably, to characterise *Tochmarc Becḟola* as 'a peculiar confused tale';[18] but I have argued that they should on the contrary be regarded as central elements in a story concerned with the fundamental 'otherness' of the realm of the *síde*.[19] Patrick Sims-Williams, while inclined to accept this analysis, has taken it a step further with the persuasive suggestion that the northern and southern locations of the island are linked by the presence in both of the cult of Saint Máedóc, who was himself connected with Devenish; and the further suggestion that Devenish may have been the place of the tale's composition.[20] Joanne Findon has been more concerned with Becḟola as a conscious and speaking subject, and with the ways in which the earlier version of the tale in particular gives her 'a voice and a mind of her own'.[21] That such a woman can find an appropriate mate only in the Otherworld may also be significant.[22]

'The chief saga of the mythological cycle', according to Dillon, is ***Cath Maige Tuired*** ('The Battle of Mag Tuired'; *CLH* §1019);[23] and this assessment would surely be echoed by many other scholars.[24] Although the story is often alluded to in the literature, and extracts from a lost copy of it have survived in at least one glossary,[25] this is another text which has come down to us in only

---

[18] *Studies in Irish Literature and History*, 229.

[19] Carey, 'Time, Space, and the Otherworld', 3–4; also 'Otherworlds and Verbal Worlds', 35–7.

[20] '*Tochmarc Becfhola*'.

[21] 'Looking for "Mr. Right"'. I have touched upon cognate questions in '*Yonec* and *Tochmarc Becḟola*'.

[22] See further Findon, 'A Good (Mortal) Man is Hard to Find'.

[23] *Early Irish Literature*, 57.

[24] Thus Ó Cuív, in Dillon, *Irish Sagas*, 32: 'If we may judge from the frequent references to it in the literature from the year 1200 on, it seems to have been the most popular tale of the so-called mythological cycle'.

[25] Pearson, 'A Medieval Glossary', §§4, 8, 74, 172. The compiler of this glossary cites other texts found in Harley MS 5280: not only *Tochmarc Emire* (§§12, 26, 29, 36, 66, etc.) but also *Baile in Scáil* and the Old Irish treatise on the Psalter (§20 and §38, otherwise attested only in Rawlinson

a single manuscript: London, BL Harley MS 5280. This single copy, moreover, lacks the conclusion.[26] As it has survived, the tale clearly has various strata: thus, to cite one of the most obvious instances, its opening paragraphs have been taken from *Lebor Gabála Érenn*.[27] Elizabeth Gray, *Cath Maige Tuired*'s most recent editor, has accepted the view of Gerard Murphy (and others) that 'it seems to be true that the story under consideration is indeed the product of an eleventh or twelfth-century redactor working mainly upon ninth-century material'.[28]

After this redactor has situated the narrative within the framework of Middle Irish pseudo-history, we are told how the conception of Bres resulted from a fleeting union between a princess of the Túatha Dé Donann, who had recently become the rulers of Ireland, and a king of the Fomoiri from beyond the sea. When Núadu was obliged to forfeit the kingship of Ireland because of the loss of an arm, Bres was chosen in his place. Bres proved however to be the epitome of a bad ruler: avaricious, guilty of false judgements, and without regard for the due ordering of society. Under his rule, the Fomoiri oppressed the Túatha Dé, the greatest of whose lords were forced to toil as slaves. At last, Bres was maneuvered into pronouncing a false judgement, following which his meanness provoked a satire from the poet Cairpre, and he was obliged to resign his rule.[29] Núadu, whose arm had been

---

MS B 512), *Táin Bó Rúanada* (§70, otherwise attested only in TCD MS 1337 and RIA MS 23.N.10 [catalogue number 967]) and *Ces Ulad* (§55, found in no other manuscript; see pp. 24–5, n. 24 above).

[26] Cf. my remarks in 'Myth and Mythography', 54–5.

[27] Murphy, 'Notes on *Cath Maige Tuired*', 195; Carey, 'Myth and Mythography', 53–4.

[28] Gray, *Cath Maige Tuired*, 11. For further arguments in support of this view, see Ó Corráin, 'The Vikings in Scotland and Ireland', 310–13. The main earlier editions and translations are Stokes, 'The Second Battle of Moytura'; Thurneysen, 'Zu irischen Texten', 401–6; and Lehmacher, 'Die zweite Schlacht von Mag Tured'.

[29] As Ó Cathasaigh has noted ('*Cath Maige Tuired*', 2–6), the false judgement and the satire are doublets, both performing the same function in the narrative. Cairpre's satire is the subject of a separate anecdote preserved in TCD MS 1336 (shelf-mark H 3.17) and the Yellow Book of Lecan (Hull, 'Cairpre mac Edaine's Satire'), besides being referred to in various medieval glossaries and in the poem *Tairgidh mo sheachna, a shíol mBriain*, ascribed to Tadhg Mac Bruaideadha and addressed to Donnchadh Ó Briain (died A.D. 1624). In this last instance, curiously, the satire is attributed not to Cairpre but to Cridenbél, another satirist of the Túatha Dé; in the view of the poem's editor, Roisin McLaughlin, this divergence can be regarded 'either as reflecting a different tradition or as representing the

magically restored, resumed the kingship. Fleeing to the land of the Fomoiri, Bres prevailed upon his father to raise an army to invade Ireland and restore him to the throne.

At this time of crisis there appeared the youthful hero Lug: a sort of opposite of Bres, having a father from the Túatha Dé and a mother from the Fomoiri. Recognising Lug's superior qualities after the youth's dramatic arrival at Tara, Núadu handed authority over to him. Himself possessed of every skill, Lug was able to coordinate the various abilities of the other Túatha Dé so as to make them into a fighting force of the greatest possible effectiveness. In the climactic battle of Mag Tuired, the Fomoiri were defeated and Bres was captured; to buy his life, he was obliged to reveal the best times for ploughing, sowing and reaping.

Since the nineteenth century, *Cath Maige Tuired* has been regarded as the reflection of a Celtic myth, itself deriving from a yet older Indo-European account of 'the War of the Gods'.[30] Comparison with material in other Celtic traditions shows that some of the narrative's central themes must indeed have a pre-Christian basis,[31] but this is by no means the key to the whole of the story. Writing in 1940, Marie-Louise Sjoestedt already remarked upon the importance in the narrative of 'circumstances which reflect [...] conditions familiar in Celtic societies, political and domestic',[32] thereby pointing in a direction which was subsequently to be explored by Gray in a series of important articles.[33] Kim

---

deliberate manipulation by the poet of his material in order to render his own threat of satire more potent' ('A Threat of Satire', 40; text at 49–50).

[30] For several references, see Carey, 'Myth and Mythography', 62 nn. 1–4. Many more could be added: see for instance Murphy, *Saga and Myth*, 17–18; and quite recently Miller, 'In Search of Indo-European Inter-Functional War'. In a posthumously published discussion, James Carney noted that *Cath Maige Tuired*, 'the most important Irish mythological tale [...], presents what must be a large part of the Irish pantheon, and the gods are assigned roles that doubtless reflect something of their pre-Christian character' ('Language and Literature to 1169', 464–5). But the evidence for such an Indo-European protomyth is problematical: not only is a polarisation of the Túatha Dé and Fomoiri not reflected in all of the sources (see pp. 10–11 above), but the opposition between *devas* and *asuras* in India, and between *Æsir* and *Vanir* in Scandinavia, appears also to be secondary. I am grateful to one of this book's anonymous readers for calling attention to this point.

[31] Thus Puhvel, 'Mythological Reflections', 378–9; Carey, 'Nōdons, Lugus, Windos', 101–7.

[32] 'Circonstances qui reflètent [...] les conditions familières aux sociétés politico-domestiques des Celtes' (*Dieux et héros des Celtes*, 14).

[33] '*Cath Maige Tuired*: Myth and Structure'.

McCone has suggested further approaches: that the story is, to a significant extent, influenced or indeed inspired by the Old Testament's account of the first kings of Israel; and/or that it 'had as an overall contemporary political message the importance of social cohesion and rallying around the Tara kingship in order to repel foreign attacks'.[34] In an article published at around the same time, I made an extended case for the explanatory power of the latter analysis, arguing that *Cath Maige Tuired* seems to be in several respects an innovative work rather than a traditional one, and that it should be understood as the creative redeployment of inherited materials in response to the social and cultural situation at the time of its composition. Following the scholarly consensus which regards the main body of the tale as being essentially a text of the ninth century, I see it as reflecting anxieties concerning traditional values at a time of cultural change, as Scandinavian influences began to affect the fabric of Irish society.[35]

[34] 'A Tale of Two Ditties', especially 136.

[35] 'Myth and Mythography'. With a considerably more specific historicist approach, and — as it seems to me — a rather selective view of what constitutes significant detail, Michael Chesnutt has argued that the story is a 'parable' of the battle of Clontarf, fought A.D. 1014 ('*Cath Maige Tuired*').

5. Lore and Fantasy in the Middle Irish Period

All of the texts considered so far appear to have been first composed in the eighth or the ninth century, perhaps in some cases in the early tenth. They were modified in the course of their transmission in the Middle Irish period, and during this period new versions of several of them were composed. There is, however, at first sight curiously little evidence of the composition of new tales concerning the Túatha Dé between the tenth and the twelfth centuries. Two notable exceptions to this generalisation are the section in *Lebor Gabála Érenn* that describes the rule over Ireland of the Túatha Dé Donann (which can itself, however, scarcely be described as a 'tale');[1] and the *dindṡenchas* narratives that have members of the Túatha Dé as their protagonists.

In ***Lebor Gabála Érenn*** ('The Book of the Taking of Ireland'; *CLH* §1141), the Túatha Dé Donann are presented as the fourth of the races to have settled Ireland after the Flood, and as the predecessors of the Gaels. The text speaks of their conquest of the island, enumerates their kings, and provides an elaborate account of their genealogy which is developed and extended in the course of the work's evolution. An essential feature of this treatment is its euhemerism. As Mark Williams observes:

> The crucial innovation of the Irish pseudo- or synthetic history lay in its explicit insistence that the Túatha Dé had been a race of men and women [...]. The importance of this development can hardly be overstated, as a basic faith in the fundamental historicity of this narrative prevailed for centuries, so that it effectively became Ireland's official framework for its native gods.[2]

For all the importance of its influence on later literature, it is also necessary to recognise that this view of the Túatha Dé never triumphed entirely. Even within *Lebor Gabála Érenn* itself, the idea that they were supernatural beings surfaces repeatedly.[3]

Besides allusions to the events of *Cath Maige Tuired*, a few

---

[1] It appears to be the *Lebor Gabála Érenn* account, rather than a story as such, which is included in the Middle Irish tale-lists as the *tochomlad* or 'migration' of the Túatha Dé Donann. Cf. discussion above, pp. 4–5.

[2] *Ireland's Immortals*, 130.

[3] Thus they are identified as 'demons' in the passage cited on p. 11 above; see further Carey, 'The Old Gods of Ireland', 56–8.

brief stories are included in *Lebor Gabála Érenn*. Thus the recension known as the *Míniugud* ('Explanation') contains, under the title *Imthechta Tuirill Picreo ⁊ a Mac* ('The Wanderings of Tuirill Picreo and his Sons'), a poem (with prose paraphrase) which tells how the three sons of Tuirill Picreo acquired several magical treasures in order to recompense Lug for the killing of his father;[4] while the second recension includes a strange story of how the Túatha Dé, before coming to Ireland, used their magic to assist the Athenians in a war against the Philistines.[5] In addition, the second recension gives a description of how the Túatha Dé formerly resided in four cities in the north of the world, where they studied magic under four masters, and from which they brought four treasures to Ireland. This account also exists as a separate and apparently autonomous tract; indeed, it is probably a version of this that was absorbed by *Lebor Gabála Érenn* as the latter evolved and expanded.[6]

The first and third recensions of *Lebor Gabála Érenn*, and the *Míniugud*, further contain the long poem *Éstid, a eólchu cen on* ('Listen, scholars without flaw'), an enumeration of the deaths of the Túatha Dé Donann composed by Flann Mainistrech (died A.D. 1056).[7] Besides information that is also found in the prose of *Lebor Gabála Érenn*, and in *Cath Maige Tuired*, Flann alludes to Lug's killing of Cermait son of the Dagda (cf. 'How the Dagda Got his Magic Staff', below); and to the deaths of Bres, Boand and Áed son of the Dagda as these are related in *dindṡenchas* anecdotes.[8] The accounts which Flann gives of the killing of

---

[4] Macalister, *Lebor Gabála Érenn*, iv, 134–7, 282–91. The text was also edited with translation by Thurneysen, 'Tuirill Bicrenn'.

[5] Ibid., 138–41.

[6] Hull, 'The Four Jewels'; cf. Macalister, *Lebor Gabála Érenn*, iv, 106–7, 142–5, 168–9. Copies are found in the Yellow Book of Lecan, the Book of Ballymote (RIA MS 23.P.12; catalogue number 536), BL Egerton MS 105 and NLI MS G 1. It may however be queried whether this item really counts as a tale, rather than as a bit of legendary lore. Another such case is the short poem *Tomus tige Mec ind Óc* ('The measurement of the house of Mac ind Óc'), a description of the house of Óengus preserved in Harley MS 5280, RIA MS B.iv.2 (catalogue number 1080) and RIA MS 23.N.10: Meyer, 'Mitteilungen aus irischen Handschriften', 108.

[7] Macalister, *Lebor Gabála Érenn*, iv, 224–41; cf. my remarks, *A Single Ray of the Sun*, 16. Williams is correct when he states that Flann's purpose in composing this poem was to insist on the Túatha Dé's mortality; I think however that he may go too far when he argues that it is 'as much satire as historical scholarship' (*Ireland's Immortals*, 184).

[8] §11 (cf. *MD* iii, 216–23; Stokes, 'The Prose Tales', §46); §15 (see references on p. 41, n. 16 below); §23 (cf. *MD* iv, 92–121; Stokes, 'The Prose Tales', §91).

Abcán by Óengus, and of the death of Midir's wife Fúamnach, differ from what we find in other sources, but can by the same token be taken to be variants of existing tales rather than mere fabrication.[9] There is accordingly good reason to presume that lost stories lie behind the other allusions in the poem.

The ***Dindṡenchas*** collections (*CLH* §1144) include dozens of tales, or allusions to tales, whose main characters belong to the Túatha Dé.[10] Some of these are so truncated that it is hard to be confident that any authentic tradition lies behind them: they may well represent no more than perfunctory *ad hoc* fabrication.[11] Others share so many characters or plot elements with better-known stories that it seems probable that they have been more or less directly based upon them.[12] Elsewhere, however, we appear to have alternative versions of tales, not merely items deriving from them: such are the accounts of the death of Bres at Carn Uí Néit,[13]

---

[9] §17 (cf. Thurneysen, 'Das Gedicht der vierzig Fragen', 132 §8); §29 (cf. Bergin and Best, 'Tochmarc Étaíne', 160, with Flann's conflicting statement cited on 188–90).

[10] This formulation is deliberately vague, as it is not clear what should be counted; but the number is certainly not less than thirty. Speaking of the *dindṡenchas* corpus as a whole, Brian Ó Cuív stated that 'legends from the so-called "Mythological Cycle" are by far the most numerous' ('*Dinnshenchas*', 103). Not all of the relevant material is in the main collections (for example, Gwynn, 'Cináed úa hArtacáin's Poem'); and the poem *Connachta cid dia tá int ainm* ('Connachta: whence is the name?'), with its account of struggles against the Túatha Dé, has not yet been critically edited (*LL* ll. 3209–76).

[11] Examples would be the association of Loch Cé with a druid of Núadu's (*MD* iii, 400–403; Stokes, 'The Edinburgh Dinnshenchas', §75), the reference to Dían Cécht's healing activity at Lusmag (*MD* iv, 182–5; Stokes, 'The Edinburgh Dinnshenchas', §71; Stokes, 'The Prose Tales', §108), the explanations offered for the name Umall (*MD* iv, 272–5), or the list of fallen warriors of the Fomoiri in the account of Slíab Badbgna (ibid., 282–3). As it happens, all of these items are ancillary to the events of *Cath Maige Tuired.*

[12] The origin-legend of Cnogba seems to have used the first part of *Tochmarc Étaíne* in this way (*MD* iii, 40–43, 483; cf. Stokes, 'The Bodleian Dinnshenchas', §43); while the account of Odras (*MD* iv, 196–201; Stokes, 'The Prose Tales', §113) appears to be indebted to *Echtra Nerai*, *Táin Bó Regamna* and *Esnada Tige Buchet*.

[13] *MD* iii, 216–23; Stokes, 'The Prose Tales', §46; as noted above, the story was already known to Flann Mainistrech. For an argument that this localisation of Bres's death may date from *c.* A.D. 1100, see Ó Murchadha, 'Carn Uí Néid'. I have discussed the episode in 'Nōdons, Lugus, Windos', 107; and it has been considered in detail by Ó hAodha, 'Carn Uí Néit agus

and of Midir's abduction of Étaín in the *dindšenchas* of Ráith Esa and Ráith Chrúachna.[14] Some anecdotes, although they are brief, contain so much curious detail that it is unlikely that they were devised merely to explain placenames: particularly conspicuous examples are the stories of battles with water monsters undertaken by Dían Cécht and the Dagda.[15] There are several versions of the story of how Boand defied the power of a magic well, and was first mutilated and then drowned by an upsurge of punishing waters which became the course of the river Boyne: it has been shown that significant elements within this account almost certainly derive from pre-Christian myth.[16] The early origins of the doublet legends describing the origins of Lough Neagh and Lough Ree, involving the actions of magical horses belonging to Óengus and Midir, are evident from the existence of a significantly older version of the former story in a poem in Oxford, Bodleian Library, Laud Misc. MS 610.[17] In this poem, however, there is by contrast with the Middle Irish tellings nothing to indicate the involvement of any of the Túatha Dé.

These remarks by no means exhaust all that could be said concerning this material: it is a rich corpus, concerning which it is impossible to generalise. It does seem safe to say, however, that the stories about the Túatha Dé composed during the Middle Irish period were for the most part either retellings of older tales, or brief anecdotes absorbed in the great systematisations of lore that are so characteristic of the time.[18] But there are a handful of

an Dindshenchas'.

[14] *MD* ii, 2–9; *MD* iii, 348–55; Stokes, 'The Bodleian Dinnshenchas', §27; Stokes, 'The Prose Tales', §§3, 65.

[15] *MD* ii, 62–3; *MD* iv, 294–5; Stokes, 'The Bodleian Dinnshenchas', §15; Stokes, 'The Prose Tales', §13. The story about the Dagda is also found in *Tochmarc Emire*, from which the *Dindšenchas* may well have derived it: van Hamel, *Compert Con Culainn and Other Stories*, 36.

[16] *MD* ii, 28–33, 36–7; Stokes, 'The Bodleian Dinnshenchas', §36; Stokes, 'The Prose Tales', §19; *Tochmarc Emire* (van Hamel, *Compert Con Culainn and Other Stories*, 37–8); Gwynn, 'Cináed úa hArtacáin's Poem', 228–9, 235–6. Discussion in Dumézil, 'Le puits de Nechtan'; cf. Carey, 'Irish Parallels'.

[17] *MD* iii, 450–59, 500; Stokes, 'The Edinburgh Dinnshenchas', §55; Stokes, 'The Prose Tales', §79; O'Grady, *Silva Gadelica*, i, 233–7; cf. Meyer, 'The Laud Genealogies', 307–8. New editions and extended analysis in de Vries, *Two Texts on Loch nEchach*.

[18] Further information can be extracted from other texts of this nature. As indicated on p. 40, n. 9 above, Eochaid ua Cérín's poem *Dúan in Chethrachat Cest* ('Poem of the Forty Questions') gives an account of how Óengus killed the *síd* musician Abcán; it also speaks of an attack made by Óengus

exceptions to this generalisation, to which we can now turn.

The short tract that begins ***Cía trēide cētna-labratar íarna genemain fo chétōir*** ('What three first spoke immediately after their birth?'; *CLH* §1024), preserved in the Yellow Book of Lecan and (missing the end of the text) in the Book of Leinster, comprises three stories, the first of which describes 'the first utterance of Aí son of Ollam'.[19] Fíachu (in other sources Fíachna) mac Delbaíth, one of the Túatha Dé Donann kings of Ireland according to the pseudo-historical scheme codified in *Lebor Gabála Érenn*, was feasting with his brother, the *fili* (poet-scholar) Ollam, when all heard a great blast of wind. The king's druid said that this wind betokened the birth of a son to Ollam's wife, whose rank would be the same as the king's; eventually an even loftier rank would come, this being the order of the church. When the child was born, Fíachu commanded that he be killed; but Ollam prevented this, and Aí then recited a poem in which he demanded from the king a series of rich gifts 'for your honour's sake' (*dot inchaib*). These gifts were granted.[20]

This little tale is a social allegory, the key to which lies in the names of the characters: *aí* is a word for poetry, while *ollam* designates an individual who has reached the highest rank in any of the professions, but most particularly a master poet. In his analysis of the text, James Carney has observed:

> It was not primarily a tale told for entertainment — indeed, it is not particularly entertaining. Its main point is that it stresses the rights owing to the learned classes by the wielders of power. By an ancient contract, going back to the Tuatha Dé Danann days [...], the king of Ireland granted sustenance to men of art, and a social position for an *ollam* equivalent to that of a king.[21]

---

upon the warriors of Emain Macha (Thurneysen, 'Das Gedicht der vierzig Fragen', 131–2 §§7–8).

[19] What Donnchadh Ó Corráin (*CLH*) has called a 'genealogical synopsis' of part of the text is edited from Oxford, Bodleian Library, Rawlinson MS B 502, with variants from three other manuscripts, in O'Brien, *Corpus Genealogiarum Hiberniae*, 188–9.

[20] Thurneysen, 'Zur keltischen Literatur', 272–3; idem, 'Die drei Kinder', 193–4.

[21] Carney, 'The Deeper Level', 170. Cf. Radner, '"Men Will Die"', 172–8; and Williams, *Ireland's Immortals*, 163–5.

A version of this story already existed in the Old Irish period: from a series of questions and answers in the section of the legal text *Bretha Nemed Déidenach* ('Second Judgements of Status') that is headed *Tuarustal nÚadh* ('Testimony of Poetry'), it appears that poetry (*aí*) was first recited by Aí son of Ollam to Fíachna son of Delbáeth, for a reward of thirty cows.[22] One element peculiar to the Middle Irish version, which must however be very old, is the wind which serves as an omen of Aí's birth. It can scarcely be a coincidence that the word *aí* itself appears to derive from an Indo-European root meaning 'to blow, to breathe'; but there is no reflection of such a putative original sense in the Irish word's attested use.[23]

The symbolic figures of Ollam and Aí are a particularly clear example of the way in which members of the Túatha Dé, in particular those associated with the arts, could figure in what Williams has characterised as 'a kind of meta-mythology for intellectuals', helping to underpin 'the *filid*'s cognitive ideology'.[24] They came however to be regarded as being just as 'real' as any of the other characters in Ireland's legendary history: Aí's death is included in Flann's poem, and Ollam's is noted in *Lebor Gabála Érenn*.[25]

The story to which Osborn Bergin gave the title **'How the Dagda Got his Magic Staff'** (*CLH* §1034) is found uniquely, in fragmentary form, in the Yellow Book of Lecan.[26] It describes how the Dagda's son Cermait was killed by Lug (here called 'high king of Ireland') in revenge for having seduced the latter's wife; the Dagda embalmed his body, and then carried it on his back into 'the eastern world'. There he met three brothers, who were engaged in dividing the 'treasures' (*seoid*) left them by their father: these were a mantle and a shirt which respectively granted their wearer the ability to change his appearance and protected him against disease; and a staff (*lorg*), one end of which brought death to the

[22] Gwynn, 'An Old-Irish Tract', 38–9. Other statements in this section suggest differences in the story: it is said that *aí* appeared to Aí in darkness and in sleep, 'in the shape of a nubile girl' (*i riocht inghine macdhacht*).

[23] Watkins, 'Indo-European Metrics', 215–16; for the root, see Pokorny, *Indogermanisches etymologisches Wörterbuch*, 81–4. It should however be noted that Watkins subsequently changed his mind about this etymology: *How to Kill a Dragon*, 117.

[24] Williams, *Ireland's Immortals*, 181, 173.

[25] Macalister, *Lebor Gabála Érenn*, iv, 124, 184.

[26] Bergin, 'How the Dagda Got his Magic Staff'.

living while the other revived the dead. The Dagda asked to be allowed to hold the staff, and immediately used it to kill the three brothers and to bring Cermait back to life. When Cermait reproached him for having slain the brothers, he restored their lives to them also, but insisted on borrowing the staff for as long as it took to 'kill his enemies with it, and revive his friends'. In this way he gained the kingship of Ireland for himself.

Cermait's affair with Lug's wife, and its fatal consequences, are mentioned in other Middle Irish sources;[27] and the Dagda's staff or *lorg* figures briefly in *Cath Maige Tuired*, while its ability to take and to restore life is described in the Book of Leinster version of the saga *Mesca Ulad*.[28] So far as I can see, it is an open question whether these texts drew upon a version of our story, or the story was itself a confection based on such traditions: the language suggests a date fairly late in the Middle Irish period. The tale's broader affiliations have not yet been investigated. On the one hand, the three brothers dividing their father's wealth are reminiscent of Cermait's own sons as they are portrayed in *Lebor Gabála Érenn*;[29] or, more distantly, of the sons of Tuirill Picreo gathering magical treasures as wergild for the bereaved Lug.[30] On the other hand, the story of a wanderer who makes his fortune when he is asked to assist in the division of property (often involving magical treasures) is well known as an international folktale.[31] The style of our narrative seems compatible with the intersection within it of popular and learned registers.

Togail Síde Truim ('The Sack of Síd Truim'), uniquely preserved in TCD MS 1337, takes up only ten lines of printed text. We are told how Bodb attacked Síd Truim,[32] and contended with its proprietor Curchán; when the struggle began to go against Bodb,

---

[27] To the references noted by Bergin, ibid., 400, may be added an allusion in a prose account of the *dindṡenchas* of Loch Lugborta (*MD* iv, 278–9); and an apologue in the poem *Cumha ceathrair do mheasg mé* ('Grief for four men has plunged me in confusion') by Cathal Mac Muireadhaigh (composed A.D. 1636; Cameron, *Reliquiæ Celticæ*, ii, 238–9). In the latter, note that the editor's rendering of *leighis le aluirg* as 'cures [...] along in his track' should be corrected to 'healing with his staff' (reading *leighis lea luirg*).

[28] Gray, *Cath Maige Tuired*, 46, l. 397; Watson, *Mesca Ulad*, 28.

[29] Macalister, *Lebor Gabála Érenn*, v, 14–17.

[30] See pp. 39 and 51.

[31] It has been designated 'Men Fight over Magic Objects' (ATU 518): Uther, *The Types of International Folktales*, i, 306–7.

[32] The importance of this *síd* is further reflected elsewhere in the literature: Hollo, 'Cú Chulainn and Síd Truim'.

his son Sárán came to his aid, and the two of them then prevailed. For all its brevity, the story is quite difficult to understand in detail: this is due to deliberate obfuscation on the part of the author, who peppers his account of the fight with such otherwise unattested words as *rabaing* and *ilping*.[33]

Any consideration of this enigmatic anecdote should take note of the fact that it is the first in a series of short items, all of which are distinguished by their obscurity. Two of these, *Tochmarc Baíse Bandruad* ('The Wooing of Báes the Druidess') and *Táin Bó Rúanada* ('The Cattle Raid of Rúanaid'), contain arcane rhythmical speeches or 'rhetorics';[34] another, *Cath Slébe Caín* ('The Battle of Slíab Caín'), resembles *Togail Síde Truim* inasmuch as it is a prose narrative without dialogue.[35] The four pieces have widely varying contexts: the speech in *Tochmarc Baíse Bandruad* is addressed to Fachtna Fáthach, said to have been the father of Conchobur mac Nesa; *Cath Slébe Caín* describes a battle between Find mac Cumaill and his arch-rival Goll mac Morna; and the background of *Táin Bó Rúanada* is unclear. One thing which the latter two have in common with one another and with *Togail Síde Truim*, however, is that all three contain accounts of combats which are rendered obscure by the use of rare or otherwise unattested terminology. These shared traits may have led the scribe, or an earlier compiler, to group them together; alternatively, some or all of them may be the work of a single author. A third possibility, which could only be tested by a closer study of all four texts, is that some may have been composed in imitation of the others. My own suspicion is that this is the case with *Togail Síde Truim*. Several of its verb forms seem to be later Middle Irish, and — by contrast with *Táin Bó Rúanada* and *Cath Slébe Caín* — the riddling words are not so far as I can see found elsewhere. These words may accordingly be fresh coinages on the part of an author lacking real familiarity with the traditional 'poetic language' (*bérla na filed*).

Between *Tochmarc Baíse Bandruad* and *Táin Bó Rúanada* there is a fifth text, which has not yet been published. Bearing the heading ***Bruigen Séinbic hIdbric*** ('The Hostel of Senbecc ua Ebricc'), this relates how Cú Chulainn encountered the diminutive

[33] Edited by Meyer, 'Mitteilungen aus irischen Handschriften', 104; tentative translation by Carey, 'Obscure Styles in Medieval Ireland', 35.

[34] Both of these texts are aso found in RIA MS 23.N.10 and in Harley MS 5280.

[35] These three texts have all been printed by Meyer, 'Mitteilungen aus irischen Handschriften', 35–6.

Túatha Dé musician Senbecc beside the Boyne, and how the latter recited a poem to him; other accounts of such meetings between Senbecc and Cú Chulainn are found in *Bretha Nemed Déidenach*, and as part of a collection of 'Ulster cycle' material in RIA MS D.iv.2.[36]

It is debatable whether stories of supernatural encounters that are set in the historical period can be assigned to a 'mythological cycle'; this doubt attaches for instance to *Tochmarc Becfola*, discussed above. Three Middle Irish instances may be noted here.

An anecdote in Liber Flavus Fergusiorum relates how the poet Mac Coise encountered a giant woman weeping beside a lake. She told him that her lover had been killed in a *síd*, and had then been buried at the church of Clonmacnoise. Mac Coise related his adventure to the king of Ireland, Congalach mac Maíle Mithig (reigned 944–956). When the monks of Clonmacnoise were asked about this, they said that they knew of no recent burial there; but a monk died shortly thereafter, and the digging of his grave led to the discovery of the corpse of a gigantic and strikingly beautiful man. The king ordered that the grave be filled in again until it had been decided what to do about this find; but when the grave was opened a second time, the body had disappeared.[37]

In the Book of Lismore and the Book of Fermoy (RIA MS 23.E.29; catalogue number 1134) there is a story, headed ***Scél Saltrach na Muice*** ('The Tale of the Pig's Psalter'; *CLH* §1076) in the latter, of a bishop named Caínchomrac who moved from Clonmacnoise to the island monastery of Inis Éndaim in Lough Ree.[38] When his monks were cooking a pig, a man emerged from the lake and informed Caínchomrac that he had come from a monastery beneath it, 'for it is not more difficult for the Lord that people should dwell beneath the waters than in other places'.[39]

---

[36] Gwynn, 'An Old-Irish Tract', 26–7; Meyer, 'Anecdota from the Stowe MS. No 992', 182–4. This entire collection of brief texts is currently being edited from TCD MS 1337 by Chantal Kobel.

[37] Meyer, 'Mitteilungen aus irischen Handschriften', 559–60; Gwynn, 'An Old Gaelic Giant Tale'. Translation and discussion in Carey, 'The Finding of Arthur's Grave'.

[38] On Caínchomrac, see Ó Corráin, 'Máel Muire the Scribe', 8–10. The tale is edited and translated from the Book of Lismore copy in O'Grady, *Silva Gadelica*, i, 87–9; ii, 94–6; and from the Book of Fermoy and from four late paper copies in Cross, '"The Psalter of the Pig"'. The Lismore text will be cited in what follows.

[39] O'Grady, *Silva Gadelica*, i, 88: *ár ní doilghi lasin Coimdhi áitrebh dháine*

The young men of the underwater monastery had transgressed, and had been transformed into swine and expelled as punishment; it was one of these youths, the son of Caínchomrac's informant, who was now over the fire. The stranger made Caínchomrac a present of his dead son's psalter, an object which was subsequently preserved at Clonmacnoise as 'the Pig's Psalter'. Caínchomrac permitted the body to be returned to the lake-people for burial, and was invited to visit the underwater monastery. Thereafter, he continued making such visits throughout his life, and we are told that there was never any 'concealment upon it for him' (*dícleith dó uirre*);[40] when he eventually disappeared, it was conjectured that he might have gone to live beneath the lake. The mysterious folk in this story are ecclesiastics; but their underwater existence, the mention of 'concealment', and their powers of shape-shifting, seem to identify them with the people of the *síde*.

The Yellow Book of Lecan and RIA MS D.iv.2 contain a brief tale to which its most recent editor has given the title ***Bó Bithblicht meic Lonáin***. This relates how the celebrated poet Flann mac Lonáin (died *c.* A.D. 920) was stranded by a storm, along with his followers, without provisions in an empty house. A 'great, savage peasant' (*aithech mór barbarda*) with a billhook came to them, and offered them his cow as food if they would promise to give him in return any cow that he would ask for. When they agreed, he slaughtered and cooked the cow, and distributed the meat to the company so that all were well fed. After a year he returned, this time with four companions: the five were menacing and abusive, and the cow that was demanded was 'a cow always in milk' (*bó bithblicht*). Flann recited a poem describing his predicament, upon which the stranger announced that this was what he had been seeking, 'for poetry is always in milk' (*ar is bithblicht in t-aircetal*); he further revealed that he was not a commoner (*bachlach*), but 'Óengus son of Boand, the Mac Óc'.[41]

This curious little story is variously reminiscent of the conclusion of the saga *Fled Bricrenn* ('Bricriu's Feast'), at which the wizard-king Cú Roí comes in the disguise of a gigantic *bachlach* to challenge the warriors of Ulster at a feast, menacing

fó na huiscibh iná isna hinadaib aili.

[40] Ibid.

[41] Clifford, 'Bó Bithblicht'. An earlier edition, without translation, is Bergin, 'A Story of Flann mac Lonáin'; the prose is translated in Flower, *The Irish Tradition*, 70–71.

them with his axe;[42] and of an anecdote in *Sanas Cormaic*, in which the 'spirit of poetry' (*poematis* [...] *spiritus*) makes a fool of the master poet Senchán Torpéist wearing the semblance of a hideous beggar.[43] Tales of incongruously disguised beings with supernatural powers, sometimes identified as belonging to the Túatha Dé, enjoyed renewed popularity in the Early Modern period.[44]

Although I believe that such anecdotes as the stories of Mac Coise, Caínchomrac and Flann mac Lonáin should be noted here, they differ sharply from the narratives that are generally assigned to a 'mythological cycle'. Apart from these, and the handful of brief texts discussed earlier in this chapter, it is striking that most of the Middle Irish tales with members of the Túatha Dé as their protagonists are reworkings, or new versions, of stories that appear to have been composed in the Old Irish period: *De Gabáil int Ṡída*, *De Chophur in Dá Muccida*, *Tochmarc Étaíne*, *Tochmarc Becḟola*, *Cath Maige Tuired*. This might suggest a circumscribed body of source material; but, as we have seen, we have the evidence of such works as *Lebor Gabála Érenn* and the *Dindṡenchas*, and especially of Flann Mainistrech's poem on the deaths of the Túatha Dé, that many more such stories were known. The reason for this state of affairs is not yet clear.

[42] Henderson, *Fled Bricrend*, 116–29.

[43] Meyer, *Sanas Cormaic*, §1059.

[44] Two examples are *Eachtra an Cheithearnaigh Chaoilriabhaigh* ('The Adventure of the Narrow-striped Kern') and *Eachtra Bhodaigh an Chóta Lachtna* ('The Adventure of the Oaf in the Grey Coat'); specimens are edited and translated in O'Grady, *Silva Gadelica*, i, 276–96; ii, 311–31. Alan Bruford proposed a date of composition in the sixteenth century for the former, and in 'the first half of the seventeenth century' for the latter (*Gaelic Folk-tales*, 153, 129). Bruford pointed out that only the copy edited by O'Grady identifies the *Ceithearnach* as Manannán (ibid., 223 n. 8); and copies of *Eachtra Bhodaigh* in which the supernatural stranger is so identified are also infrequent. Charles MacQuarrie notes this circumstance but believes nevertheless that these figures were understood to be Manannán in all cases, suggesting that 'an audience schooled in Irish tradition would be likely to guess who the character was meant to be' (*The Biography of the Irish God of the Sea*, 302). For references to manuscript and oral versions, see Bruford, *Gaelic Folk-tales*, 252–3.

6. The Later Tradition

Several further tales concerning the Túatha Dé were composed in the later Middle Ages. To a greater or lesser extent, most of these can be seen to depend heavily on the earlier literature; but some of them developed this inherited material in intriguing ways.[1]

Two stories are directly derived from the pseudo-historical lore concerning the Túatha Dé Donann: from *Lebor Gabála Érenn*, and from the Middle Irish redaction of *Cath Maige Tuired* (which itself, as we have seen, incorporated material from *Lebor Gabála Érenn*).

A manuscript of the seventeenth century (RIA MS 24.P.9; catalogue number 739) contains the unique copy of an Early Modern Irish retelling of *Cath Maige Tuired* (*CLH* §1020). Brian Ó Cuív, in his edition of this text, commented on 'its stilted bombastic style and its artificially archaic language'; and he noted the difficulties involved in attempting to determine its date with any exactitude. He held however that 'it would seem not unlikely that our version was descended from an original compiled some centuries earlier'.[2]

The story follows its predecessor in many points of plot, and even in the stylistic device of incorporating obscure rhythmical speeches or 'rhetorics' in the narrative. There are however several important differences as well, such as the fates meted out to the tyrant Bres and to Lug's monstrous grandfather Balor.[3] While the older form of the tale is mainly concerned with the events leading up to the battle, from Bres's conception onward, the later version concentrates on the battle itself. In addition to the 'rhetorics', the account is embellished with a series of ornate speeches delivered by the leaders on both sides: these correspond to nothing in the earlier telling, and presumably have their ultimate inspiration in the Irish translations of such Latin epics as Vergil's *Aeneid* and Lucan's *Pharsalia*.[4]

---

[1] For the sake of consistency throughout the volume, I have in this chapter followed the conventions of Old Irish spelling in rendering the names of persons and places (but not the titles of texts); I regret any resulting incongruities.

[2] *Cath Muighe Tuireadh*, 13, 17.

[3] The main discrepancies between the versions are listed by Ó Cuív, ibid., 5–8.

[4] With Lug's speech to the Túatha Dé, ibid. 29–30, may, for example, be compared the speeches of Aeneas and Turnus to their troops: Calder,

As noted above, a case can be made for seeing the Old Irish *Cath Maige Tuired* as a parable of the cultural politics of the ninth century. Similarly, Mícheál Hoyne has argued that its Early Modern Irish successor was inspired by a battle fought, at Mag Tuired, between two groups of Connacht lords in the year 1398, and that it was written specifically as propaganda for the Meic Dhiarmada of Moylurg.[5] The story finds a different application in the poem *Mór ar bfearg riot a rí Saxan* ('Great our anger toward you, king of the English'), composed by Gofraidh Fionn Ó Dálaigh in the interval A.D. 1356–1358: here it is not a Gaelic prince but a young Anglo-Norman lord, Maurice Fitz Maurice earl of Desmond, who is compared to Lug entering Tara shortly before the great battle; and Núadu's court serves as a counterpart to that of Edward III in London.[6]

The pseudo-historical tradition distinguishes between the battle fought at Mag Tuired between the Túatha Dé Donann and the Fomoiri, in which Lug defeated Bres, and an earlier battle of Mag Tuired, fought between the Tuatha Dé Donann and their kinsmen the Fir Bolg for control over Ireland. The latter is narrated in a tale preserved in TCD MS 1319 (shelf-mark H 2.17), the work of at least two scribes; there are fragments of another version in UCD-OFM MS A 33 (*CLH* §1018).[7] In the remarks which introduce his edition, John Fraser suggested that 'we have here the result of several revisions of a text which may, in parts, go back to the early MIr. period'.[8] But I am not aware of any evidence that directly supports such an assessment, while there is at least one indication to the contrary: the tale includes a poem from *Lebor Gabála Érenn* containing some readings that are otherwise found only in the copy of that work in the Book of Ballymote (fourteenth-

Imtheachta Æniasa, 154.

[5] Hoyne, 'The Political Context of *Cath Muighe Tuireadh*', accordingly dates the tale significantly later than Murphy, who had surmised that it 'was first written down probably in the thirteenth century' (*Saga and Myth*, 20).

[6] Bergin, *Irish Bardic Poetry*, 73–81, 244–8. There are some differences of detail between the story here and that in *Cath Maige Tuired*: Lug boasts of various feats of agility not attributed to him in the older tale, and enters Tara by leaping; and he states that he has come to Ireland from the Otherworldly island of Emain Ablach. With this last point, cf. the statement in *Oidheadh Chloinn Tuireann* that Lug had come from the Otherworld realm of Tír Tairngire (Ua Ceallaigh, *Trí Truagha na Scéaluidheachta*, 7).

[7] The latter are edited in Ó Cuív, 'Fragments of a Modern Irish Version of the First Battle of Magh Tuireadh'.

[8] 'The First Battle of Moytura', 3.

fifteenth century), not even in the closely related copy in the Great Book of Lecan.[9]

The author of this story distinguishes himself by his extensive knowledge of lore concerning the settlements of Ireland; and he goes into considerable detail in his account of how the ancestors of the Túatha Dé Donann and Fir Bolg were obliged to leave Ireland, and of the adventures and wanderings of those peoples that led up to their return.[10] In what he says of the battle itself, his sympathies seem to be evenly divided between the two sides. After the death of the Fir Bolg king Eochaid (in which overwhelming thirst plays a role, a motif probably drawn from *Togail Bruidne Da Derga*),[11] it is at last agreed that the Túatha Dé Donann will exercise rule over the greater part of Ireland but will cede Connacht to the Fir Bolg. It is interesting that Bres is portrayed positively throughout. At one point he is said to be the brother of the Dagda and of Ogma: this was evidently the original doctrine concerning him, but it is one which is expressly denied in the Old Irish *Cath Maige Tuired* and in most subsequent texts.[12]

Another tale that takes the battle of Mag Tuired as one of its points of departure is ***Oidheadh Chloinne Tuireann*** ('The Death of the Children of Tuirenn'; *CLH* §1077). Mention has been made above (p. 39) of a story, summarised in one of the versions of *Lebor Gabála Érenn*, of how the three sons of Tuirill Bicreo were obliged by Lug to go in quest of a series of magical treasures as recompense for having killed Lug's father Cían; in Flann Mainistrech's poem on the deaths of the Túatha Dé Donann, it is stated that they were themselves killed by Lug, on the Isle of Man.[13] Placing these incidents against the backdrop of the great battle, a later author constructed a grim story of revenge and tragedy. The tale begins however, rather inconsequentially, with an account of how Núadu's arm was restored to him: not, as in *Cath Maige Tuired*, by one of his own physicians, but by three strangers. The

---

[9] This is a brief composition enumerating the wives of the leaders who brought the Fir Bolg to Ireland: ibid., 16–17 and Macalister, *Lebor Gabála Érenn*, iv, 46–7. Only our tale and the Ballymote copy of *Lebor Gabála Érenn* call the fifth wife *Liben* (*Liber* in all other copies).

[10] Even more on these subjects was originally present in the tale; but there is a gap in the manuscript at this point.

[11] Knott, *Togail Bruidne Da Derga*, 42–4.

[12] Fraser, 'The First Battle of Moytura', 46–9. For Bres as brother of the Dagda and Ogma, see discussion in Carey, 'Myth and Mythography', 56–7.

[13] Macalister, *Lebor Gabála Érenn*, iv, 232–3.

same individuals also give a second eye to Núadu's one-eyed gatekeeper.[14] With this, the narrative moves to the preparations for the great battle.

Cían, seeking aid for his son Lug in the impending conflict with the Fomoiri, stumbled upon the sons of Tuirenn (clearly identical with the sons of Tuirill in the older story). As hereditary enemies of his kindred, they murdered him, and presently the crime was discovered. In imposing the blood-price upon the culprits, Lug claimed that he would use the treasures to gain victory over the enemy; but the battle itself forms no part of the story, and Lug's ultimate aim in setting the brothers such a series of perilous tasks was to bring about their deaths. They were indeed successful in accomplishing all that had been asked of them, due largely to a combination of trickery and wholesale violence; but they were mortally wounded in carrying out the final exploit, and died as a consequence of Lug's refusal to forgive his enemies even after they had made the covenanted payment.[15]

The oldest manuscript of the tale was written in A.D. 1684.[16] It is generally grouped together with *Oidheadh Chloinne Lir* ('The Death of the Children of Lir', of which more below) and *Oidheadh Chloinne Uisnigh* ('The Death of the Children of Uisneach'; a late version of the Ulster cycle tale *Loinges Mac nUislenn*). That these three are often transmitted together, and are referred to collectively as *Trí Truagha na Scéalaigheachta* ('The Three Sorrows of Storytelling'), has led some scholars to suggest that all three might be the work of a single author; but since both the grouping and the designation appear to go back only to the eighteenth century, this hypothesis seems implausible.[17] An eccentric Latin version of the opening portion of the story, apparently composed early in the seventeenth century by one Hugh Casserly, is found on some paper leaves bound at the front of Harley MS 5280.[18] A poem by Gofraidh Fionn Ó Dálaigh (died A.D. 1387) alludes to the fall of

[14] Diarmuid Johnson sees in Núadu and his gatekeeper counterparts for the pair of blemished deities whom Dumézil designated 'dieu manchot' and 'dieu borgne': 'Go bhfios dom, is é OCT an t-aon áit amháin a bhfuil an mhóitif seo ar mharthain i litríocht na Gaeilge' ('*Oidhe Chloinne Tuireann*', 80). Johnson here undertakes to correct Dumézil himself, who had withdrawn an earlier suggestion that Irish legend affords evidence of such a pairing: '"Le borgne"'.

[15] Ua Ceallaigh, *Trí Truagha na Scéaluidheachta*, 5–41.

[16] Johnson, '*Oidhe Chloinne Tuireann*', 78.

[17] Breatnach, 'The Religious Significance', 1–2, 32.

[18] Text and discussion in Gray, 'Early Seventeenth-century Tracts'.

the sons of Tuirenn on Cnoc Mac Midchaín:[19] as this is a climactic episode in *Oidheadh Chloinne Tuireann*, and one to which nothing in the Middle Irish evidence corresponds, it appears likely that our tale goes back at least to the fourteenth century.[20]

This indication of date has led Caoimhín Breatnach to suggest that the story was written as an 'exemplary myth', rather like *Cath Maige Tuired* several centuries earlier. In the present case, however, the *exemplum*'s message is a negative one. By portraying the Túatha Dé Donann as riven by feuds and vengeance the author has, in Breatnach's view, alluded to a contemporary situation: the self-destructive rivalry of the great Anglo-Norman lordships during the reigns of the first Edwards.[21] Whatever about the details of this hypothesis — and it is one that Breatnach advances very tentatively — there can be no doubt that he is correct in calling attention to the problematical darkness of the picture which the tale presents to us.

Oidheadh Chloinne Lir, like *Oidheadh Chloinne Tuireann*, is attested mainly in manuscripts of the eighteenth and nineteenth centuries. The oldest surviving copy appears to be that in Edinburgh, National Library of Scotland MS Adv. 72.1.38 (formerly Advocates' Library Gaelic MS XXXVIII), dated to the sixteenth or the early seventeenth century; and the story is mentioned in a document that seems to have been written around 1500.[22] The tale relates how a dispute between two lords of the *síde*, Bodb Derg son of the Dagda and Lir of Síd Finnachaid, is resolved when Bodb bestows his fosterdaughter Áeb on Lir as a wife.[23] Áeb bears Lir two sets of twins — a daughter named

[19] Mac Cionnaith, *Dioghluim Dána*, 194; this allusion's significance for dating has been noted by Breatnach, '*Oidheadh Chloinne Tuireann*', 43.

[20] Contrast Williams's view, for which however he gives no grounds, that *Oidheadh Chloinne Tuireann* is 'probably a composition of the 1500s'. He also proposes that it can in part be regarded as 'a deliberate parallel to the Labours of Hercules' (*Ireland's Immortals*, 260, 265).

[21] Breatnach, '*Oidheadh Chloinne Tuireann*'.

[22] Breatnach, 'The Religious Significance', 2.

[23] It is uncertain to what extent Bodb Derg son of the Dagda is a version of Bodb of Síd ar Ḟemun, mentioned occasionally in Old and Middle Irish literature (thus pp. 21, 23, 44–5 above). In *Lebor Gabála Érenn*, the latter is said to be son of Echu Garb (for example, *LL* l. 1185), rather than of the Dagda. In the Early Modern Irish *Cath Fionntrágha*, on the other hand, Bodb Derg son of the Dagda is found at 'Síd Ban Finn above Mag Femen' (*Sith Bhan Ḟinn os Feimeanmuidh*: Meyer, *Cath Finntrága*, 13–14). The earliest explicit mention of Bodb Derg known to me is in a list of the sons

Finngúala, and three sons named Áed, Fíachra and Conn — but dies in the course of her second labour. Lir then marries Áeb's sister Aífe; but she becomes jealous of her stepchildren and transforms them into swans. They are condemned to spend three periods, of three centuries each, in three different locations;[24] during this time they experience grievous suffering, and the brothers are repeatedly comforted by Finngúala. At last they come under the protection of Saint Mocháemóc, and eventually regain a human appearance. But now they are shrivelled with age; and they die immediately after having gained assurance of salvation through their acceptance of baptism.[25]

The background of the story has been variously assessed. James Carney noted resemblances between the tribulations of the children of Lir and those experienced by the legendary forest-dwelling madman Suibne Geilt, holding indeed that 'the tale OCL is, to a large extent, based upon [...] the twelfth century tale known to us as *Buile Suibhne*'.[26] In a detailed recent study, Caoimhín Breatnach has acknowledged these similarities but proposes a considerably more sophisticated reading of the narrative. In his view, its main thrust is devotional, with evocations of the sufferings of sinful souls and of the vanity of worldly pleasures contrasting with the abiding joys of heaven. He suggests that the author may have been a Franciscan, perhaps writing in Westmeath in the later fifteenth century.[27]

It is evident that the story as we have it is a late composition;[28] and the spiritual concerns of the later Middle Ages, as well

---

of the Dagda in a *dindṡenchas* anecdote uniquely preserved in RIA MS D.ii.2 (catalogue number 1222): *Aedh ⁊ Cermad caem ⁊ Aenghus ⁊ Midir aite Aenghusa ⁊ Bodb Derg* (*MD* iv, 268). For insightful discussion of Bodb Derg's depiction in the later literature, see Williams, *Ireland's Immortals*, 221–34, 255–7.

24 These locations vary to some extent in different versions of the tale: details in Breatnach, 'The Religious Significance', 4–7.

25 Text in Ua Ceallaigh, *Trí Truagha na Scéaluidheachta*, 42–64. For references to other editions, see Breatnach, 'The Religious Significance', 2 n. 11; in n. 8 he states that he is at work on an edition of his own.

26 *Studies in Irish Literature and History*, 153.

27 'The Religious Significance', especially 37–40.

28 This can be readily seen from the name *Lir* itself, which is not so far as I know attested before the Early Modern Irish period. It is in fact not originally a name at all, but a petrified genitive of the common noun *lear* 'sea', extracted from Manannán's epithet *Mac Lir* 'Son of the Sea'. Cf. Vendryes, 'Manannan Mac Lir'; Williams, *Ireland's Immortals*, 254–5 (and, for the observation that Lir is 'the most papery and undeveloped figure in the whole pantheon', 259). The argument of M.E. Dobbs that 'the

as descriptions of privation in *Buile Ṡuibne*, may well have influenced the author. But account must also be taken of two other sources: international folktales, and earlier stories concerning the Túatha Dé.

The folktale type with which *Oidheadh Chloinne Lir* can most readily be compared is that which has been designated 'The Maiden Who Seeks Her Brothers' (ATU 451): here a group of brothers are transformed (often into swans) by a stepmother, but eventually restored thanks to the self-sacrificing heroism of their sister (we may be reminded here of the protective role assumed by Finngúala).[29] There are several further tales in medieval Irish which involve the metamorphosis of an innocent victim, transformed in these cases not by a stepmother but by a rival wife or lover: besides *Tochmarc Étaíne*, noted above, there is a story of how one *síd*-woman changed another into a crane, which then lived for two hundred years in the house of Manannán; and another of a woman whose rival (said in one version to be a 'fairy mistress') changed her into a dog.[30] The many centuries of Étaín's sufferings after she has become a fly are especially reminiscent of the ordeal of the children of Lir. Comparable elements are also apparent in the story of Lí Ban, a princess who is changed into a fish or mermaid, and wanders the seas for three centuries until she finds baptism and a pious death in the care of saintly clerics. Like Finngúala, Lí Ban recites a poem describing her transformed existence and remembering happier days.[31]

Late and in many respects innovative as it is, therefore, *Oidheadh Chloinne Lir* can be seen to be dependent at every level on traditions and tales concerning the Túatha Dé which can be traced back into the Middle Irish and indeed the Old Irish periods.

Altram Tighe Dá Mheadar ('The Fosterage of the House of Two Vessels'; *CLH* §988), the last story to be considered in this survey, survives only in the Book of Fermoy; but a poem lamenting the heroine's death, which Saint Patrick is made to utter at the tale's conclusion, is preserved in various later manuscripts.[32] The narrative

story originated in Connaught between 650 and 770' ('The Date and Shaping of Oidhe Chlainne Lir', 236) can be cited only as a curiosity.

29 Uther, *The Types of International Folktales*, i, 267–8.

30 References and discussion in Carey, 'Werewolves in Medieval Ireland', 38–40.

31 De Vries, *Two Texts on Loch nEchach*, 204–15. The parallel with Lí Ban is noted by Williams, *Ireland's Immortals*, 258.

32 Duncan, 'Altram Tige Dá Medar', 185–6; MacNeill, 'The Legends of the

begins by relating how, after the Túatha Dé Donann have been defeated by the Gaels, Manannán grants them invisibility and immortality, and allots *síde* throughout Ireland to them as dwellings; subsequently, he instructs Óengus Óc in the stratagem which enables him to wrest possession of Bruig na Bóinne from his fosterfather Elcmar. Shortly thereafter a girl named Eithne is born to the steward, and is taken in fosterage by Óengus. Years later, an insulting remark by Óengus's brother induces such a paroxysm of shame that Eithne's 'guardian demon' (*deman comuidechta*) is driven out of her,[33] and an angel takes its place. Henceforth she can no longer eat the food of the *síde*, and subsists on the milk of two cows — one belonging to Óengus, and one to Manannán — which had been brought from the 'righteous land' of India: her consumption of this milk is the 'fosterage of the house of two vessels'. After the coming of the Faith to Ireland, Eithne becomes separated from her companions and is taken under the protection, first of a cleric named Cesán, and subsequently of Patrick himself. Patrick refuses to restore her to Óengus; she then asks the saint to baptise her, and dies a fortnight thereafter.[34]

The account of Óengus's seizure of Bruig na Bóinne is comparable in various ways to *De Gabáil int Ṡída* and to the first episode of *Tochmarc Étaíne*; but there are important differences as well, at least some of which appear to antedate the story in its present form.[35] Intriguingly, essential elements in the portrayal of

---

False God's Daughter'. MacNeill is primarily interested in the explanatory stories that, in some of the modern copies, accompany the poem: these bear some resemblance to the medieval tale, but only at a very considerable remove.

33 For further examples of 'guardian demons' in Irish sources, see *Dá Brón Flatha Nime* ('The Two Sorrows of the Kingdom of Heaven'; *LU* l. 1379: *demon comaitechta*); the second recension of *In Tenga Bithnúa* ('The Ever-new Tongue'; Carey, *In Tenga Bithnua*, 180: *demhna coimidechta*); and an anecdote concerning Solomon (*LL* ll. 36589–90: *satan comaitechta*). Williams, *Ireland's Immortals*, 242 n. 147, points out that the guardian demon already figures in the early Greek apocryphal text *The Shepherd of Hermas* vi.2.1; here it is stated that 'there are two angels in a man, one of righteousness and one of vice' (δύο εἰσὶν ἄγγελοι μετὰ τοῦ ἀνθρώπου, εἷς τῆς δικαιοσύνης καὶ εἷς τῆς πονηρίας; Funk, *Die apostolischen Väter*, 173).

34 Duncan, 'Altram Tige Dá Medar'; another edition by Dobbs, 'Altromh Tighi Dá Medar'. An extended discussion of Manannán's role in the story, together with some speculation concerning the tale's structure and background, are provided by MacQuarrie, *The Biography of the Irish God of the Sea*, 97–126; the most detailed study of the text, which I have not yet seen, is Dahl Hambro, 'Waiting for Christian Fish'.

35 Discussion in Carey, 'Time, Memory, and the Boyne Necropolis', 25–6

Eithne herself seem to be drawn from hagiography: a partial basis for her has been plausibly found in the princess Eithne, daughter of Lóegaire mac Néill, who is said to have died immediately following her baptism by Patrick;[36] and her subsistence on milk rather than on the food of the Túatha Dé recalls the inability of Brigit in the so-called *Vita prima Brigitae* to stomach the food of the druid in whose house she is living, for which she substitutes the milk of a white cow.[37] But traditions of a supernatural Eithne must lie at the roots of the tale all the same. As Clare Dagger has pointed out, the circumstance that Eithne is both reared and buried beside the Boyne can scarcely be dissociated from the statements in other sources that Eithne was the name of Elcmar's wife, or even of the tutelary Boand herself;[38] and she suggests that Eithne's burial at the ecclesiastical site *Cell Eithne* 'is simply another way of saying that the Boyne area was of particular significance as a centre of Christian worship, an area with which the goddess Eithne was also closely associated'.[39]

More than any of the other tales which have been discussed above, *Altram Tighe Dá Mheadar* is concerned with the relationship between Christianity and the native supernatural:[40] not only does it tell how Eithne received a guardian angel even during her time within the *síd*, and recount her rejection of her former life for the sake of salvation, but the beginning of the story includes a discourse by Manannán on the superiority of the One God to the gods of the pagan Irish. Similar preoccupations can be recognised in such probably more or less contemporary texts as *Acallam na Senórach* ('The Colloquy of the Old Men') or *Eachtra Thaidhg mheic Céin* ('The Adventure of Tadc mac Céin'),[41] and in the

---

and n. 9.

[36] Duncan, 'Altram', 184; for the story, see, for example, Tírechán (cited on p. 9 above); also Mulchrone, *Bethu Phátraic*, 63–5. Even a contrast between Patrick and 'men of the *síd*' is as we have seen already present in the earlier account.

[37] Colgan, *Triadis thaumaturgae ... acta*, 528 col. a; cf. Ó hAodha, *Bethu Brigte*, 2. A further comparison with Étaín is proposed by Williams, *Ireland's Immortals*, 236.

[38] Dagger, 'Eithne Ban-dia agus Ban-naomh', 68.

[39] Dagger, 'Eithne: The Sources', 116.

[40] This aspect of the story is discussed at some length by Williams, who is engaged on a more extended study of the topic: *Ireland's Immortals*, 234–46.

[41] I have examined the ontological status of the Túatha Dé in the *Acallam* in '*Acallam na Senórach*: A Conversation between Worlds'; an analysis with an analogous approach is advanced in Williams, *Ireland's Immortals*, 199–

conclusion of the somewhat earlier *Scél na Fír Flatha* ('Tale of the Ordeals of Sovereignty'):[42] for whatever reason, the place of the Túatha Dé in a Christian Ireland came once more to be the subject of frequent reflection in the later Middle Ages.

234. For *Eachtra Thaidhg*, see the aspects of the tale noted in my remarks in *A Single Ray of the Sun*, 36; and 'The Old Gods of Ireland', 61–2.

[42] Stokes, 'The Irish Ordeals', 202; see p. 16 above.

7. Conclusion

I have given considerable attention, in the course of this study, to the problems inherent in positing a 'mythological cycle' as part of the taxonomy of medieval Irish literature. As we have seen, it is unclear what should be included in such a grouping; and I expect that another scholar, undertaking such a survey, would arrive at a different selection — perhaps a very different selection — from that which is offered here. And when such stories are identified, as often as not, the tradition itself has its own ways of classifying them: as *remscéla*, for example, or as pseudo-historical lore. These difficulties of categorisation are important. If confronted thoughtfully, they can help us to appreciate the inscrutability of the Túatha Dé themselves: beings who are so essential to Irish narrative, and at the same time so elusive.

Even if the medieval Irish never conceived of the stories about the Túatha Dé as constituting a 'cycle', let alone a 'mythological' one, such an examination as has been undertaken here indicates how extensive a body of literature was devoted to the people of the *síde* between the seventh and the seventeenth centuries, a literature drawing on multitudinous traditions both popular and learned. Supernatural entities certainly figure in other medieval literatures; and Iceland in particular produced what could, with considerably more justice than is the case for Ireland, be called a 'mythological cycle'. Nevertheless, I am aware of nothing that can really be compared with the stories that we have been considering. The ambiguous nature of the Túatha Dé, their complex genealogies, their rootedness in the fabric of the landscape, their potency as symbols and personifications, and the vividness with which some of them emerge as narrative protagonists: all these elements show how crucial, and how far-ranging, was their place in the inner world of the Gael.

Bibliography

Arbois de Jubainville, H. d', *Introduction à l'étude de la littérature celtique* (Paris, 1882).

— 'Rapport sur une mission littéraire dans les Îles-Britanniques', *Archives des Missions Scientifiques et Littéraires*, 3rd Series, 10 (1883) 141–98.

— *Essai d'un catalogue de la littérature épique de l'Irlande, précédé d'une étude sur les manuscrits en langue irlandaise conservés dans les Îles Britanniques et sur le continent* (Paris, 1883).

— *Le cycle mythologique irlandais et la mythologie celtique* (Paris, 1884).

— *The Irish Mythological Cycle and Celtic Mythology*, trans. R.I. Best (Dublin, 1903).

Backhaus, N., 'The Structure of the List of *Remscéla Tána Bó Cualngi* in the Book of Leinster', *CMCS* 19 (Summer 1990) 19–26.

Baumgarten, R., *Bibliography of Irish Linguistics and Literature 1942–71* (Dublin, 1986).

Bergin, O., 'A Story of Flann mac Lonáin', *Anecdota from Irish Manuscripts* 1 (1907) 45–50.

— 'How the Dagda Got his Magic Staff', in R.S. Loomis (ed.), *Mediaeval Studies in Memory of Gertrude Schoepperle Loomis* (Paris, 1927) 399–406.

Bergin, O., and R.I. Best, 'Tochmarc Étaíne', *Ériu* 12 (1934–8) 137–96.

Bernardus Silvestris, *Cosmographia*, ed. P. Dronke (Leiden, 1978).

Best, R.I., *Bibliography of Irish Philology and of Printed Irish Literature to 1912* (Dublin, 1913).

— *Bibliography of Irish Philology and Manuscript Literature: Publications 1913–1941* (Dublin, 1942).

Best, R.I., and O. Bergin, *Lebor na hUidre: Book of the Dun Cow* (Dublin, 1929).

Best, R.I., et al., *The Book of Leinster formerly Lebar na Núachongbála*, 6 vols (Dublin, 1954–1983).

Bhreathnach, M., 'A New Edition of Tochmarc Becfhola', *Ériu* 35 (1984) 59–91.

Bieler, L., *The Patrician Texts in the Book of Armagh*, Scriptores Latini Hiberniae 10 (Dublin, 1979).

Blažek, V., 'Celto-Slavic Parallels in Mythology and Sacral Lexicon', in S. Mac Mathúna and M. Fomin (eds), *Parallels between Celtic and Slavic*, Studia Celto-Slavica 1 (Coleraine, 2006) 75–85.

Bondarenko, G., *Studies in Irish Mythology* (Berlin, 2014).

Borsje, J., 'Monotheistic to a Certain Extent: The "Good Neighbours" of God in Ireland', in A.-M. Korte and M. de Haardt (eds), *The Boundaries of Monotheism: Interdisciplinary Explorations into the Foundations of Western Monotheism*, Studies in Theology and Religion 13 (Leiden and Boston, 2009) 53–82.

Breatnach, C., 'The Religious Significance of *Oidheadh Chloinne Lir*', *Ériu* 50 (1999) 1–40.

— '*Oidheadh Chloinne Tuireann* agus *Cath Maige Tuired*: Dhá Shampla de Mhiotas Eiseamláireach', *Éigse* 32 (2000) 35–46.
Breatnach, L., 'Review of S. Mac Mathúna, *Immram Brain*', *Celtica* 20 (1988) 177–92.
Bruford, A., *Gaelic Folk-tales and Mediæval Romances: A Study of the Early Modern Irish 'Romantic Tales' and their Oral Derivatives* (Dublin, 1969).
Calder, G., *Imtheachta Æniasa: The Irish Æneid*, ITS 6 (London, 1903; repr. 1995).
Cameron, A., *Reliqiuiæ Celticæ: Texts, Papers, and Studies in Gaelic Literature and Philology*, 2 vols (Inverness, 1892–4).
Carey, J., 'The Name "Tuatha Dé Danann"', *Éigse* 18:2 (1981) 291–4.
— 'The Location of the Otherworld in Irish Tradition', *Éigse* 19:1 (1982) 36–43.
— 'Irish Parallels to the Myth of Odin's Eye', *Folklore* 94 (1983) 214–18.
— 'Nodons in Britain and Ireland', *ZCP* 40 (1984) 1–22.
— 'Time, Space, and the Otherworld', *PHCC* 7 (1987) 1–27.
— 'Sequence and Causation in *Echtra Nerai*', *Ériu* 39 (1988) 67–74.
— 'Ireland and the Antipodes: The Heterodoxy of Virgil of Salzburg', *Speculum* 64 (1989) 1–10.
— 'Myth and Mythography in *Cath Maige Tuired*', *Studia Celtica* 24/25 (1989–90) 53–69.
— 'Otherworlds and Verbal Worlds in Middle Irish Narrative', *PHCC* 9 (1990) 32–42.
— 'The Irish "Otherworld": Hiberno-Latin Perspectives', *Éigse* 25 (1991) 154–9.
— 'The Waters of Vision and the Gods of Skill', *Alexandria* 1 (1991) 163–85.
— 'A *Tuath Dé* Miscellany', *Bulletin of the Board of Celtic Studies* 39 (1992) 24–45.
— New introduction to the reprint of R.A.S. Macalister (ed.), *Lebor Gabála Érenn: The Book of the Taking of Ireland*, 5 vols, ITS 34–5, 39, 41, 45 (London, 1993) i, [1]–[21].
— 'Time, Memory, and the Boyne Necropolis', *PHCC* 10 (1993) 24–30.
— 'On the Interrelationships of Some *Cín Dromma Snechtai* Texts', *Ériu* 46 (1995) 71–92.
— 'Obscure Styles in Medieval Ireland', *Mediaevalia* 19 (1996) 23–39.
— 'The Finding of Arthur's Grave: A Story from Clonmacnoise?', in J. Carey, J.T. Koch and P.-Y. Lambert (eds), *Ildánach Ildírech: A Festschrift for Proinsias Mac Cana* (Andover and Aberystwyth, 1999) 1–14.
— 'Varieties of Supernatural Contact in the Life of Adamnán', in J. Carey, M. Herbert and P. Ó Riain (eds), *Studies in Irish Hagiography: Saints and Scholars* (Dublin, 2001) 49–62.
— 'Nōdons, Lugus, Windos', in C.M. Ternes and H. Zinser (eds), *Dieux des Celtes / Götter der Kelten / Gods of the Celts* (Luxembourg, 2002) 99–126.
— 'Werewolves in Medieval Ireland', *CMCS* 44 (Winter 2002) 37–72.

— 'Fomoiri', in J.T. Koch (ed.), *Celtic Culture, A Historical Encyclopedia*, 5 vols (Santa Barbara, Denver and Oxford, 2006) 762.
— 'From David to Labraid: Sacral Kingship and the Emergence of Monotheism in Israel and Ireland', in K. Ritari and A. Bergholm (eds), *Approaches to Religion and Mythology in Celtic Studies* (Newcastle, 2008) 2–27.
— *In Tenga Bithnua: The Ever-new Tongue*, Apocrypha Hiberniae II: Apocalyptica 1, Corpus Christianorum Series Apocryphorum 16 (Turnhout, 2009).
— 'Donn, Amairgen, Íth and the Prehistory of Irish Pseudohistory', *Journal of Indo-European Studies* 38 (2010) 319–41.
— 'Eine keltische Schicksalsgöttin?', in S. Zimmer (ed.), *Kelten am Rhein: Akten des dreizehnten Internationalen Keltologiekongresses, Zweiter Teil: Philologie — Sprachen und Literaturen* (Mainz am Rhein, 2010) 29–32.
— *A Single Ray of the Sun: Religious Speculation in Early Ireland* (2nd ed.: Aberystwyth, 2011).
— '*Dee* "Pagan Deity"', *Ériu* 62 (2012) 33–42.
— 'Ogmios and the Eternal Word', *Cosmos* 30 (2014) 1–35.
— '*Acallam na Senórach*: A Conversation between Worlds', in A. Doyle and K. Murray (eds), *In Dialogue with the Agallamh: Essays in Honour of Seán Ó Coileáin* (Dublin, 2014) 76–89.
— '*Yonec* and *Tochmarc Becfola*: Two Female *Echtrai*', in J. Carey, K. Murray and C. Ó Dochartaigh (eds), *Sacred Histories: A Festschrift for Máire Herbert* (Dublin, 2015) 73–85.
— 'The Old Gods of Ireland in the Later Middle Ages', in K. Ritari and A. Bergholm (eds), *Understanding Celtic Religion: Revisiting the Pagan Past* (Cardiff, 2015) 51–68.
— 'The Final Transformation of Étaín', *Ériu* 66 (2016) 31–8.
— 'Ireland, Wales, and Faerie: The Otherworld of Romance and the Celtic Literatures', in G. Stanivucovic (ed.), *Timely Voices: Romance Writing in English Literature* (Montreal, 2017) 140–58.
— 'Time, Identity and the Otherworld: A Note on *The Wooing of Étaín*', in E. Lyle (ed.), *Celtic Myth in the 21st Century: The Gods and their Stories in a Global Perspective*, New Approaches to Celtic Religion and Mythology (Cardiff, 2018) 23–9.
Carey, J., E. Nic Cárthaigh and C. Ó Dochartaigh (eds), *The End and Beyond: Medieval Irish Eschatology*, 2 vols (Aberystwyth, 2014).
Carney, J., *Studies in Irish Literature and History* (Dublin, 1955).
— 'The Deeper Level of Irish Literature', *Capuchin Annual* 36 (1969) 160–71.
— 'Language and Literature to 1169', in D. Ó Cróinín (ed.), *A New History of Ireland: I. Prehistoric and Early Ireland* (Oxford, 2005) 451–510.
Chadwin, T., 'The *Remscéla Tána Bó Cualngi*', *CMCS* 34 (Winter 1997) 67–75.
Charles-Edwards, T.M., '*Tochmarc Étaíne*: A Literal Interpretation', in M. Richter and J.-M. Picard (eds), *Ogma: Essays in Celtic Studies in Honour of Próinséas Ní Chatháin* (Dublin, 2002) 165–81.

Chesnutt, M., '*Cath Maige Tuired*: A Parable of the Battle of Clontarf', in S. Ó Catháin and P. Lysaght (eds), *Northern Lights: Following Folklore in North-western Europe. Essays in Honour of Bo Almqvist* (Dublin, 2001) 22–33.
Clarke, M., 'The Lore of the Monstrous Races in the Developing Text of the Irish *Sex Aetates Mundi*', *CMCS* 63 (Summer 2012) 15–49.
Clifford, D., 'Bó Bithblicht meic Lonán: Eagrán de Scéal faoi Fhlann mac Lonán', *Celtica* 25 (2007) 9–39.
Colgan, J., *Triadis thaumaturgae... acta* (Louvain, 1647; repr. Dublin, 1997).
Corthals, J., *Táin Bó Regamna: Eine Vorerzählung zur Táin Bó Cúailnge*, Sitzungsberichte Österreichische Akademie der Wissenschaften, Philosophisch-historische Klasse 478, Veröffentlichungen der Keltischen Kommission 5 (Vienna, 1987).
Cross, T.P., '"The Psalter of the Pig", an Irish Legend', *Modern Philology* 18:8 (1920) 443–55.
Dagger, C., 'Eithne Ban-dia agus Ban-naomh', *Léachtaí Cholm Cille* 15 (1985) 61–78.
— 'Eithne: The Sources', *ZCP* 43 (1989) 84–124.
Dahl Hambro, C., 'Waiting for Christian Fish on Milk from India: A Textual and Contextual Analysis of Altram Tige Dá Medar ("The Nourishment of the House of Two Milk Vessels")', unpublished Ph.D. thesis (University of Oslo, 2013).
de Vries, R., *Two Texts on Loch nEchach: De Causis Torchi Corc' Óche and Aided Echach maic Maireda*, ITS 65 (London, 2012).
Dillon, M., 'The Wooing of Becfhola and the Stories of Cano son of Gartnán', *Modern Philology* 42 (1945) 11–17.
— *The Cycles of the Kings* (Oxford, 1946).
— *Serglige Con Culainn*, MMIS 14 (Dublin, 1953).
— (ed.), *Irish Sagas* (Dublin, 1959).
— *Early Irish Literature* (repr. Dublin, 1994).
Dillon, M., and N.K. Chadwick, *The Celtic Realms* (New York, 1967).
Dinneen, P.S., *Foclóir Gaedhilge agus Béarla* (Dublin, 1927).
Dobbs, M.E., 'The Battle of Findchorad', *ZCP* 14 (1923) 395–420.
— 'Altromh Tighi Dá Medar', *ZCP* 18 (1929) 189–230.
— 'The Date and Shaping of Oidhe Chlainne Lir', *Journal of the Royal Society of Antiquaries of Ireland* 79 (1949) 236–7.
Donahue, C., 'Grendel and the *Clanna Cain*', *Journal of Celtic Studies* 1 (1950) 167–75.
Downey, C., 'Cúán ua Lothcháin and the Transmission of the *Dindṡenchas*', in A. Ó Corráin and G. Ó Riain (eds), *Celebrating Sixty Years of Celtic Studies at Uppsala University: Proceedings of the Eleventh Symposium of Societas Celtologica Nordica*, Studia Celtica Upsaliensia 9 (Uppsala, 2013) 45–61.
Draak, M., *Schimmen van het wester-eiland: Verkenningen in de Keltische traditie van het oude Ierland* (Amsterdam, 1977).
Dröge, Ch., 'Ein irischer *saṃsāra*? Betrachtungen zur Frage der "keltischen Seelenwanderungslehre"', *ZCP* 39 (1982) 261–8.

Duignan, L., *The Echtrae as an Early Irish Literary Genre* (Rahden, 2011).
Dumézil, G., 'Le puits de Nechtan' *Celtica* 6 (1963) 50–61.
— *Mythe et épopé*, 3 vols (Paris, 1968–73).
— '"Le borgne" and "le manchot": The State of the Problem', in G.J. Larson (ed.), *Myth in Indo-European Antiquity* (Berkeley, 1974) 17–28.
Dumville, D.N., '*Echtrae* and *Immram*: Some Problems of Definition', *Ériu* 27 (1976) 73–94.
Duncan, L., 'Altram Tige Dá Medar', *Ériu* 11 (1932) 184–225.
Egeler, M., *Walküren, Bodbs, Sirenen: Gedanken zur religionsgeschichtlichen Anbindung Nordwesteuropas an den mediterranen Raum*, Ergänzungsbände zum Reallexikon der Germanischen Altertumskunde 71 (Berlin and New York, 2011).
Evelyn-White, H.G., *Hesiod, the Homeric Hymns and Homerica*, Loeb Classical Library 57 (London and New York, 1914).
Findon, J., 'Looking for "Mr. Right" in *Tochmarc Becfhola*', in S. Sheehan and A. Dooley (eds), *Constructing Gender in Medieval Ireland* (New York, 2013) 57–74.
— 'A Good (Mortal) Man is Hard to Find: Fand, Macha, Becfhola and Bad Romance', in M.B. Ó Mainnín and G. Toner (eds), *Ulidia 4: Proceedings of the Fourth International Conference on the Ulster Cycle of Tales* (Dublin, 2017) 116–28.
Flower, R. *Catalogue of Irish Manuscripts in the British Museum*, vol. 2 (London, 1926).
— *The Irish Tradition* (Oxford, 1947).
Fogarty, H., '*Aislinge Óenguso*: A *Remscél* Reconsidered', in J.F. Eska (ed.), *Narrative in Celtic Tradition: Essays in Honor of Edgar M. Slotkin*, CSANA Yearbook 8–9 (Colgate NY, 2011) 56–67.
Fraser, J., 'The First Battle of Moytura', *Ériu* 8 (1915–16) 1–63.
Funk, F.X., *Die apostolischen Väter* (Tübingen and Leipzig, 1901).
Gervase of Tilbury, *Otia Imperialia: Recreation for an Emperor*, ed. and trans. S.E. Banks and J.W. Binns (Oxford, 2002).
Gray, B., 'Reading *Aislinge Óenguso* as a Christian-Platonist Parable', *PHCC* 24/25 (2004–5) 16–39.
Gray, E.A., 'Early Seventeenth-century Tracts in Harleian 5280', *Journal of Celtic Studies* 3 (1981–2) 136–64.
— *Cath Maige Tuired: The Second Battle of Mag Tuired*, ITS 52 (Naas, 1982).
— '*Cath Maige Tuired*: Myth and Structure', *Éigse* 18 (1981) 183–209; 19 (1982–3) 1–35, 230–62.
Gwynn, E.J., *The Metrical Dindshenchas*, Todd Lecture Series 8–12, 5 vols (Dublin, 1903–35).
— 'An Old-Irish Tract on the Privileges and Responsibilities of Poets', *Ériu* 13 (1942) 13–60.
Gwynn, L., 'The Two Versions of Tochmarc Étaíne', *ZCP* 9 (1913) 353–6.
— 'Cináed úa hArtacáin's Poem on Brugh na Bóinne', *Ériu* 7 (1914) 210–38.
— 'An Old Gaelic Giant Tale', *The Irish Monthly* 42:497 (November 1914) 640–45.

— 'The Recensions of the Saga "Togail Bruidne Da Derga"', *ZCP* 10 (1915) 209–22.

Hall, A., *Elves in Anglo-Saxon England: Matters of Belief, Health, Gender and Identity*, Anglo-Saxon Studies 8 (Woodbridge, 2007).

Hamp, E., 'The Dag(h)d(h)ae and his Relatives', in L. Sawicki and D. Shalev (eds), *Donum Grammaticum: Studies in Latin and Celtic Linguistics in Honour of Hannah Rosén*, Orbis Supplementa 18 (Leuven, 2001) 163–9.

Henderson, G., *Fled Bricrend: The Feast of Bricriu*, ITS 2 (London, 1899).

Herbert, M., '*Fled Dúin na nGéd*: A Reappraisal', *CMCS* 18 (Winter 1989) 75–87.

Hollo, K., 'Cú Chulainn and Síd Truim', *Ériu* 49 (1998) 13–22.

Hoyne, M., 'The Political Context of *Cath Muighe Tuireadh*, the Early Modern Irish Version of the Second Battle of Magh Tuireadh', *Ériu* 63 (2013) 91–116.

Hull, V., 'Cairpre mac Edaine's Satire upon Bres mac Eladain', *ZCP* 18 (1929) 63–9.

— 'The Four Jewels of the Túatha Dé Danann', *ZCP* 18 (1929) 73–89.

— '*De Gabáil in t-Ṡída* (Concerning the Seizure of the Fairy Mound)', *ZCP* 19 (1931) 53–8.

— 'Ces Ulad', *ZCP* 29 (1962–4) 305–14.

Johnson, D., '*Oidhe Chloinne Tuireann*: Ársaíocht, Aithris agus Athnuachan', in D. Ó Baoill, D. Ó hAodha and N. Ó Muraíle (eds), *Saltair Saíochta, Sanasaíochta agus Seanchais: A Festschrift for Gearóid Mac Eoin* (Dublin, 2013) 78–82.

Knott, E., *Togail Bruidne Da Derga*, MMIS 8 (Dublin: DIAS, 1936).

Lehmacher, G., 'Die zweite Schlacht von Mag Tured und die keltische Götterlehre', *Anthropos* 26 (1931) 435–59.

— 'Der Dagde, das Haupt der irischen Götter', *Anthropos* 48 (1953) 817–36.

Lewis, C.S., *The Discarded Image: An Introduction to Medieval and Renaissance Literature* (Cambridge, 1964).

Macalister, R.A.S., *Lebor Gabála Érenn*, 5 vols, ITS 34–5, 39, 41, 45 (London, 1938–56; repr. 1993).

Mac Cana, P., *The Learned Tales of Medieval Ireland* (Dublin, 1980).

Mac Cionnaith, L., *Dioghluim Dána* (Dublin, 1938).

Mac Mathúna, S., *Immram Brain: Bran's Journey to the Land of the Women*, Buchreihe der Zeitschrift für celtische Philologie 2 (Tübingen 1985).

— 'The Relationship of the Chthonic World in Early Ireland to Chaos and Cosmos', in J. Borsje, A. Dooley, S. Mac Mathúna and G. Toner (eds), *Celtic Cosmology: Perspectives from Ireland and Scotland* (Toronto, 2014) 53–76.

MacNeill, M., 'The Legends of the False God's Daughter', *Journal of the Royal Society of Antiquaries of Ireland* 79:1/2 (1949) 100–109.

— *The Festival of Lughnasa* (Oxford, 1962).

MacQuarrie, C.W., *The Biography of the Irish God of the Sea from The Voyage of Bran (700 A.D.) to Finnegans Wake (1939): The Waves of Manannán* (Lewiston, Queenston and Lampeter, 2004).

Maher, M., 'De Gabáil int Ṡída: An Edition and Literary Analysis', unpublished MA thesis (National University of Ireland, 2012).
— '*De Gabáil int Ṡída*: *Remscél* or *Remremscél*?', in M.B. Ó Mainnín and G. Toner (eds), *Ulidia 4: Proceedings of the Fourth International Conference on the Ulster Cycle of Tales* (Dublin, 2017) 150–61.
Maier, B., 'Dead Men Don't Wear Plaid: Celtic Myth and Christian Creed in Medieval Irish Concepts of the Afterlife', in J.F. Nagy (ed.), *Writing Down the Myths*, Cursor Mundi 17 (Turnhout, 2013) 107–36.
McCone, K., 'A Tale of Two Ditties: Poet and Satirist in *Cath Maige Tuired*', in D. Ó Corráin et al. (eds), *Sages, Saints and Storytellers: Celtic Studies in Honour of Professor James Carney* (Maynooth, 1989) 122–43.
— *Echtrae Chonnlai and the Beginnings of Vernacular Narrative Writing in Ireland*, Maynooth Medieval Irish Texts 1 (Maynooth, 2000).
McLaughlin, R., 'A Threat of Satire by Tadhg (Mac Dáire) Mac Bruaideadha', *Ériu* 55 (2005) 37–57.
Meid, W., *Die Suche nach der Traumfrau. Aislinge Óenguso: Oengus' Traum. Eine altirische Sage*, Innsbrucker Beiträge zur Kulturwissenschaft, Neue Folge 14 (Innsbruck, 2017).
Meyer, K., 'Macgnimartha Find', *RC* 5 (1881–3) 197–204.
— 'Anecdota from the Stowe MS. No 992', *RC* 6 (1883–5) 173–86.
— *Cath Finntrága*, Medieval and Modern Irish Series 1:4 (Oxford, 1885).
— 'The Adventures of Nera', *RC* 10 (1889) 212–28.
— 'Uath Beinne Etair', *RC* 11 (1890) 125–34.
— 'Die irisch-gälische Literatur', in H. Zimmer et al. (eds), *Die romanischen Literaturen und Sprachen mit Einschluß des Keltischen*, Die Kultur der Gegenwart, Teil I, Abteilung 11:1 (Berlin and Leipzig, 1909) 79–95.
— *Sanas Cormaic: An Old-Irish Glossary ... Edited from the Copy in the Yellow Book of Lecan*, *Anecdota from Irish Manuscripts* 4 (Halle and Dublin, 1912).
— 'The Laud Genealogies and Tribal Histories', *ZCP* 8 (1912) 291–338.
— 'Mitteilungen aus irischen Handschriften', *ZCP* 8 (1912) 102–20, 195–232, 559–65.
— 'Zur keltischen Wortkunde V', *Sitzungsberichte der Königlich Preussischen Akademie der Wissenschaften* (1914) 630–42.
— 'Ein altirischer Heilsegen', *Sitzungsberichte der Königlich Preussischen Akademie der Wissenschaften* (1916) 420–22.
McKenna, C., 'Apotheosis and Evanescence: The Fortunes of Saint Brigit in the Nineteenth and Twentieth Centuries', in J.F. Nagy (ed.), *The Individual in Celtic Literatures*, CSANA Yearbook 1 (Dublin, 2001) 74–108.
Miller, D.A., 'In Search of Indo-European Inter-Functional War', in J. Greppin and E.C. Polomé (eds), *Studies in Honor of Jaan Puhvel*, Part Two: *Mythology and Religion*, JIES Monograph 21 (Washington DC, 1997) 205–27.
Mommsen, Th., 'Historia Brittonum cum additamentis Nennii', *Monumenta Germaniae Historica, Auctores antiquissimi* 13, *Chronica minora saec. IV. V. VI. VII.* iii (Berlin, 1898) 111–222.

Mulchrone, K., *Bethu Phátraic: The Tripartite Life of Patrick* (Dublin, 1939).

Müller-Lisowski, K., 'Contributions to a Study in Irish Folklore: Traditions about Donn', *Béaloideas* 18 (1948) 142–99.

Murphy, G., 'Notes on *Cath Maige Tuired*', *Éigse* 7 (1953–5) 191–8.

— *Saga and Myth in Ancient Ireland* (Dublin, 1961).

Murray, K., *Baile in Scáil: The Phantom's Frenzy*, ITS 58 (London, 2004).

Ní Bhrolcháin, M., *An Introduction to Early Irish Literature* (Dublin, 2009).

Ní Shéaghdha, N., *Tóruigheacht Dhiarmada agus Ghráinne: The Pursuit of Diarmaid and Gráinne*, ITS 48 (Dublin, 1967).

O'Brien, M.A., *Corpus Genealogiarum Hiberniae*, vol. 1 (Dublin, 1962).

Ó Cathasaigh, T., 'The Semantics of *Síd*', *Éigse* 17:2 (1977–8) 137–55.

— 'The Theme of Lommrad in Cath Maige Mucrama', *Éigse* 18:2 (1981) 211–24.

— '*Cath Maige Tuired* as Exemplary Myth', in P. de Brún et al. (eds), *Folia Gadelica: Essays Presented by Former Students to R.A. Breatnach* (Cork, 1983) 1–19.

— 'Knowledge and Power in *Aislinge Óenguso*', in A. Ahlqvist and V. Čapková (eds), *Dán do Oide: Essays in Memory of Conn R. Ó Cléirigh* (Dublin, 1997) 431–8.

— '*Tochmarc Étaíne* II: A Tale of Three Wooings', in P. O'Neill (ed.), *The Land Beneath the Sea: Essays in Honour of Anders Ahlqvist's Contribution to Celtic Studies in Australia*, Sydney Series in Celtic Studies 14 (Sydney, 2013) 129–42.

Ó Coileáin, S., '*Echtrae Nerai* and its Analogues', *Celtica* 21 (1990) 155–76.

Ó Corráin, D., 'The Vikings in Ireland and Scotland in the Ninth Century', *Peritia* 12 (1998) 296–339.

— 'Máel Muire the Scribe: Family and Background', in R. Ó hUiginn (ed.), *Lebor na hUidre*, Codices Hibernenses Eximii 1 (Dublin, 2015) 1–28.

— *Clavis Litterarum Hibernensium*, Corpus Christianorum Claves 1 (Turnhout, 2017).

Ó Cuív, B., *Cath Muighe Tuireadh: The Second Battle of Magh Tuireadh* (Dublin, 1945).

— 'Fragments of a Modern Irish Version of the First Battle of Magh Tuireadh', *Celtica* 1:1 (1946) 111–17.

— '*Dinnshenchas* — The Literary Exploitation of Irish Place-names', *Ainm* 4 (1989–90) 90–106.

O Daly, M., *Cath Maige Mucrama: The Battle of Mag Mucrama*, ITS 50 (Dublin, 1975).

Ó Duilearga, S., 'Nera and the Dead Man', in J. Ryan (ed.), *Féil-sgríbhinn Eóin Mhic Néill* (Dublin, 1940) 522–34.

Ó Flaithearta, M., '*Echtra Nerai*, *Táin Bó Regamna* und ihr Verhältnis zur *Táin Bó Cúailnge*', in H.L.C. Tristram (ed.), *Deutsche, Kelten und Iren. 150 Jahre deutsche Keltologie: Gearóid Mac Eoin zum 60. Geburtsag gewidmet* (Hamburg, 1990) 155–76.

O'Grady, S.H., *Silva Gadelica (I-XXXI): A Collection of Tales in Irish with Extracts Illustrating Persons and Places*, 2 vols (London, 1892).

Ó hAodha, D., *Bethu Brigte* (Dublin, 1978).

Ó hAodha, T., 'Carn Uí Néit agus an Dindshenchas', unpublished MA thesis (National University of Ireland, 2014).

Ó Mainnín, M., *Place-Names of Northern Ireland*, vol. 3: *County Down III: The Mournes* (Belfast, 1993).

— 'Eochaid Ua Flainn agus Eochaid Ua Flannucáin: Súil Úr ar an bhFianaise', *Léann* 2 (2009) 75–105.

Ó Murchadha, D., 'Carn Uí Néid', *Dinnseanchas* 5:4 (Nollaig 1973) 101–13.

Ó Murchú, L.P., 'D'Uaithne Ó Mórdha a Thit i gCath 17ú Lúnasa 1600', in J. Carey, M. Herbert and K. Murray (eds), *Cín Chille Cúile — Texts, Saints and Places: Essays in Honour of Pádraig Ó Riain* (Aberystwyth, 2004) 334–53.

O'Rahilly, C., *Táin Bó Cúailnge: Recension I* (Dublin, 1976).

Pearson, A.I., 'A Medieval Glossary', *Ériu* 13 (1942) 61–87.

Pokorny, J., *Indogermanisches etymologisches Wörterbuch* (Bern and Stuttgart, 1959).

Poppe, E., *Of Cycles and Other Critical Matters: Some Issues in Medieval Irish Literary History and Criticism*, E.C. Quiggin Memorial Lecture 9 (Cambridge, 2008).

Puhvel, J., 'Mythological Reflections of Indo-European Medicine', in G. Cardona, H.M. Hoenigswald and A. Senn (eds), *Indo-European and Indo-Europeans: Papers Presented at the Third Indo-European Conference at the University of Pennsylvania* (Philadelphia, 1970) 369–82.

Quin, E.G. (gen. ed.), *Dictionary of the Irish Language: Based Mainly on Old and Middle Irish Materials*, compact edition (Dublin, 1983).

Radner, J.N., '"Men Will Die": Poets, Harpers, and Women in Early Irish Literature', in A.T.E. Matonis and D.F. Melia (eds), *Celtic Language, Celtic Culture: A Festschrift for Eric P. Hamp* (Van Nuys, 1990) 172–86.

Rees, A., and B. Rees, *Celtic Heritage: Ancient Tradition in Ireland and Wales* (London and New York, 1961).

Roberts, B.F., *Cyfranc Lludd a Llefelys*, Mediaeval and Modern Welsh Series 7 (Dublin, 1975).

Rodway, S., 'Mermaids, Leprechauns, and Fomorians: a Middle Irish Account of the Descendants of Cain', *CMCS* 59 (Summer 2010) 1–17.

Roider, U., *De Chophur in Da Muccida: wie die beiden Schweinehirten den Kreislauf der Existenzen durchwanderten*, Innsbrucker Beiträge zur Sprachwissenschaft 28 (Innsbruck, 1979).

Rose, H.J., and S. Hornblower, 'Euhemerus', in S. Hornblower and A. Spawforth (eds), *The Oxford Classical Dictionary*, 3rd rev. ed. (Oxford, 2003) 567.

Sayers, W., 'Bargaining for the Life of Bres in *Cath Maige Tuired*', *Bulletin of the Board of Celtic Studies* 34 (1986) 26–40.

— 'Netherworld and Otherworld in Early Irish Literature', *ZCP* 59 (2012) 201–30.

Shaw, F., *The Dream of Óengus: Aislinge Óenguso* (Dublin, 1934).

Sims-Williams, P., '*Tochmarc Becfhola*: A "Peculiar Confused Tale"?', in J.F. Eska (ed.), *Narrative in Celtic Tradition: Essays in Honor of Edgar M. Slotkin*, CSANA Yearbook 8/9 (Hamilton NY, 2011) 228–34.

— *Irish Influence on Medieval Welsh Literature* (Oxford, 2011).
Sjoestedt, M.-L., *Dieux et héros des Celtes* (Paris, 1940).
Stokes, W., 'The Irish Ordeals, Cormac's Adventure in the Land of Promise, and the Decision as to Cormac's Sword', *Irische Texte* 3:1 (1891) 183–229.
— 'The Second Battle of Moytura', *RC* 12 (1891) 52–130, 306–8.
— 'The Bodleian Dinnshenchas', *Folklore* 3 (1892) 467–516.
— 'The Edinburgh Dinnshenchas', *Folklore* 4 (1893) 471–97.
— 'The Prose Tales in the Rennes Dindšenchas', *RC* 15 (1894) 272–336 and 418–84; 16 (1895) 31–83, 135–67, 269–312.
— 'The Annals of Tigernach: The Fourth Fragment, A.D. 973–A.D. 1088', *RC* 17 (1896) 337–420.
— 'Acallamh na Senórach', *Irische Texte* 4:1 (1900).
— 'The Death of Crimthann son of Fidach, and the Adventures of the Sons of Eochaid Muigmedón', *RC* 24 (1903) 172–207.
Stokes, W., and J. Strachan, *Thesaurus Palaeohibernicus: A Collection of Old-Irish Glosses Scholia Prose and Verse*, 2 vols (Cambridge, 1901–3).
Theuerkauf, M-L., 'A Note on *Sect.o.f.n.*', *Celtica* 29 (2017) 76–89.
Thurneysen, R., 'Tuirill Bicrenn und seine Kinder', *ZCP* 12 (1918) 239–50.
— 'Zur keltischen Literatur und Grammatik', *ZCP* 12 (1918) 271–89.
— 'Zu irischen Texten', *ZCP* 12 (1918) 398–407.
— *Die irische Helden- und Königsage bis zum 17. Jahrhundert* (Halle, 1921).
— 'Das Gedicht der vierzig Fragen von Eochaid ua Cērīn', *ZCP* 13 (1921) 130–36.
— 'Die drei Kinder, die gleich nach ihrer Geburt sprachen', *ZCP* 20 (1936) 192–204.
Toner, G., 'Mythological Cycle', in S. Duffy (ed.), *Medieval Ireland: An Encyclopedia* (New York and London, 2005) 348–50.
— 'Narrative, Death and the Otherworld in *Echtra Nera*', in G. Toner and S. Mac Mathúna (eds), *Ulidia 3: Proceedings of the Third International Conference on the Ulster Cycle of Tales* (Berlin, 2013) 107–20.
Tovar, A., 'The God *Lugus* in Spain', *Bulletin of the Board of Celtic Studies* 29 (1982) 591–9.
Ua Ceallaigh, S., *Trí Truagha na Scéaluidheachta* (Dublin, 1927).
Uther, H.-J., *The Types of International Folktales: A Classification and Bibliography*, Folklore Fellows Communications 284–6, 3 vols (Helsinki, 2004).
van Hamel, A.G., *Lebor Bretnach: The Irish Version of the Historia Britonum Ascribed to Nennius* (Dublin, 1932).
— *Compert Con Culainn and Other Stories*, MMIS 3 (Dublin, 1933).
Vendryes, J., 'Manannan Mac Lir', *ÉC* 7 (1952–4) 239–54.
— *Airne Fíngein*, MMIS 15 (Dublin, 1953).
Watkins, C., 'Indo-European Metrics and Archaic Irish Verse', *Celtica* 6 (1963) 194–249.
— *How to Kill a Dragon: Aspects of Indo-European Poetics* (Oxford, 1995).
Watson, A., 'A Structural Analysis of *Echtra Nerai*', *ÉC* 23 (1986) 129–42.

Watson, J.C., *Mesca Ulad*, MMIS 13 (Dublin, 1941).

White, N., *Compert Mongáin and Three Other Early Mongán Tales*, Maynooth Medieval Irish Texts 5 (Maynooth, 2006).

Wiley, D.M., 'Mythological Cycle', in J.T. Koch (ed.), *Celtic Culture, A Historical Encyclopedia*, 5 vols (Santa Barbara, Denver and Oxford, 2006) 1326–8.

— 'An Introduction to the Early Irish King Tales', in D.M. Wiley (ed.), *Essays on the Early Irish King Tales* (Dublin, 2008) 13–67.

Williams, J.E.C., and P.K. Ford, *The Irish Literary Tradition* (Belmont MA, 1992).

Williams, M., *Ireland's Immortals: A History of the Gods of Irish Myth* (Princeton, 2016).

Wooding, J. (ed.), *The Otherworld Voyage in Early Irish Literature: An Anthology of Criticism* (Dublin, 2000).

General Index

—A—
Abcán 40–41
Acallam na Senórach 4, 57
Adam 15, 17
Áeb 53
Áed son of Lir 54
Áed son of the Dagda 39, 54
Aeneas 49
Æsir 11, 36
Aí 42–3
Aífe 54
Ailill Ánguba 30
Ailill mac Mátach 21–22, 25–7
Airne Fíngein 8, 13, 23
Aislinge Óenguso **20–22**, 23, 31–2
Altram Tighe Dá Mheadar 20, **55–7**
Ana 16
angel(s) 15–16, 56–7
asuras 11, 36
Athenians 39
Augustine of Hippo, *City of God* 31

—B—
Baile in Scáil 8, 17, 34
Balor 49
Becḟola 32–4
Bernardus Silvestris, *Cosmographia* 17–18
Bethu Brigte 57
Bethu Phátraic 12–13, 57
Bible 5
Bó Bithblicht Meic Lonáin **47–8**
Boand 21, 29, 31, 39, 41, 47, 57
Bodb Derg son of the Dagda 53–4
Bodb of Síd ar Ḟemun 21–3, 32, 44–5, 53–4
Boyne 41, 46, 57
Bres 35–6, 39–41, 49–51
Bretha Nemed Déidenach 42, 46
Brí Léith 27, 30–31
Brian Bóruma 12
Brigantia 10
Brigit (goddess) 10, 16
Brigit (saint) 10, 57
Brión 27
Bruig na Bóinne 21, 29, 56
Bruigen Séinbic hIdbric 25, **45–6**
Buile Ṡuibne 54–5

—C—
Cáer Ibormeith 21
Caínchomrac 46–8
cairddes 19, 23, 32
Cairpre 35
Carn Uí Néit 40–41
Casserly, Hugh 53
Cath Findchorad 22
Cath Fionntrágha 53–4
Cath Maige Mucrama 27
Cath Maige Tuired (Early Modern Irish) **49–50**
Cath Maige Tuired (Old/Middle Irish) 7, 10–11, 14, **34–7**, 38–40, 44, 48–53
Cath Slébe Caín 45
Cell Eithne 57
Cermait son of the Dagda 39, 43–4, 54
Ces Ulad 24–5, 35
Cesán 56
Cía trēide cētna-labratar íarna genemain fo chétōir **42–3**
Cían 51–2
Clonmacnoise 46
Clontarf 37
Cnoc Mac Midchaín 53
Cnogba 40
Compert Mongáin 8
Conaire Már 6, 30, 32
Conchobur mac Nesa 1–2, 21, 45
Congalach mac Maíle Mithig 46
Conn Cétchathach 17

Conn son of Lir 54
Connachta cid dia tá int ainm 40
Cormac mac Airt 16–17
Cormac mac Cuilennáin 16
Cridenbél 35
Crúachan, *see also* Ráith Chrúachna 25
Cú Chulainn 1–2, 4, 14, 25–6, 46
Cú Roí 47
Curchán 45
Cyfranc Lludd a Lleuelys 24
Cypria 28

—D—

Dá Brón Flatha Nime 56
Dagán, *see also* Dagda 19
Dagda, *see also* Dagán 8, 10, 12, 14, 16, 19, 21, 29, 31–2, 39, 41, 43–4, 51, 53–4
De Chophur in Dá Muccida **22–4**, 25, 31–2, 48
De Gabáil int Ṡída 14, **19–20**, 23, 29, 31–2, 48, 57
dee 9
demon(s) 11, 15–16, 38, 56
devas 10, 36
Devenish 33–4
Dían Cécht 12, 40–41
Díarmait mac Áedo Sláine 32–3
Díarmait ua Duibne 8
Dinas Emrys 24
dindṡenchas 5–7, 30, 34, 38–41, 44, 54
Dindṡenchas 5–6, **40–41**, 48
Domangart mac Echach 13
Donn Cúailnge 21, 26–7
Donn Fírinneach 13–14
draci 18

—E—

Eachtra an Cheithearnaigh Chaoilriabhaigh 48
Eachtra Bhodaigh an Chóta Lachtna 48
Eachtra Thaidhg mheic Céin 57–8
Echtra Nerai 8, 16, **24–7**, 31–2, 40
Echtrae Chonnlai 11, 14
echtrai 8, 27
Echu Garb 53
Edward III 50
Eithliu 17
Eithne daughter of Díchu 56–7
Eithne daughter of Lóegaire 57
Eithne wife of Elcmar 57
Elcma(i)r(e) 25, 56–7
elves 15
Emain Ablach 50
Emain Macha 42
Eochaid Airem 6, 27, 29–30
Eochaid mac Eirc 51
Eochaid ua Cérín, *Dúan in Chethrachat Cest* 21–2, 41–2
Eochaid ua Flainn 15
Eochaid ua Flannucáin 15
Esnada Tige Buchet 40
Étaín 6, 27, 29–31, 33, 41, 57
euhemerism 5, 15–16, 38
Eve 15

—F—

Fachtna Fáthach 45
fadae 18
fairies 13–14, 18
fées 14, 18
Feidelm 25
Ferry, Jules 1
Fíachna/Fíachu mac Delbaíth 42–3
Fíachra son of Lir 54
fian 4
fianaigecht 4
fianṡruth Find 4
fidchell 30
fili(d) 16, 42–3, 45
Find mac Cumaill 1–2, 4, 45
Findbennach 26
Finngúala daughter of Lir 54–5
Fir Bolg 50–51
Fir Dé 10, 19

'First Battle of Mag Tuired' **50–51**
Fitz Maurice, Maurice 50
Flann mac Lonáin 47–8
Flann Mainistrech, *Éistid, a eólchu cen on* 39–40, 43, 48, 51
Fled Bricrenn 47
Flidais 12
Fomoiri 10–11, 13, 35–6, 40, 50, 52
'Four Jewels of the Túatha Dé Donann' 39
Franciscans 54
Friuch 23
Fúamnach 29, 40

—G-J—
Genesis 4
Gervase of Tilbury, *Otia Imperialia* 18
God 9, 46, 57
gods 1–4, 6–7, 9–12, 14–16, 38, 57
Goibniu 12
Goll mac Morna 45
Ham son of Noah 11
Hercules 53
Historia Brittonum 15, 24
Homer, *Iliad* 28
Honorius, *Elucidarium* 15
'How the Dagda Got his Magic Staff' 39, **43–4**
Immram Brain 14, 22
immrama 8
Imtheachta Æniasa 49–50
Imthechta Tuirill Picreo ⁊ a Mac 39
India 56
Inis Éndaim 46
Isidore of Seville 31
Israel 37
jinn 18
Jupiter 31

—L—
lamiae 18
Lebor Bretnach 10, 15
Lebor Gabála Érenn 4–5, 7, 10–11, 35, **38–40**, 42–4, 48–51, 53
Lí Ban 55
Liber 51
Lir 53–5
Lludd 24
Loch Cé 40
Loch Lugborta 44
Lóegaire mac Néill 57
Loinges Mac nUislenn 52
'Lore of the Fiery Arrow' 21
Lough Neagh 41
Lough Ree 41, 46
Lucan, *Pharsalia* 49
Lug 8, 10, 17, 36, 39, 43–4, 49–52
Lugaid Mac Con 27
Lugus 10
Lusmag 40

—M—
Mac Bruaideadha, Tadhg, *Tairgidh mo sheachna, a shíol mBriain* 35
Mac Coise 46, 48
Mac (ind) Óc, *see also* Óengus Óc 19–21, 29, 32, 39, 47
Mac Muireadhaigh, Cathal, *Cumha ceathrair do mheasg mé* 44
Macgnímartha Finn 14
Máedóc 34
Mag Tuired 36, 50–51
Manannán 8, 16, 22, 48, 55–7
Medb 21–2, 25–7
Meic Dhiarmada 50
Mesca Ulad 8, 13, 44
Midir 29–31, 40–41, 54
Míl, sons of 19
Míniugud 39
Mocháemóc 54

Mongán mac Fíachnai 22
Mongḟind 12–13
Morrígain 26

—N-R—
Nár 23
Néit 16
Nemed 10
Nera 25–7
Newgrange, *see also* Síd in Broga 12, 20
Nōdons 10
Núadu 10, 35–6, 40, 50–52
Ó Briain, Donnchadh 35
Ó Dálaigh, Gofraidh Fionn 50, 52
Ochall 22
Odras 40
Óengus Óc, *see also* Mac (ind) Óc 8, 12, 21, 40–42, 47, 54, 56
Ogma 10, 51
Ogmios 10
Oidheadh Chloinne Lir 52, **53–5**
Oidheadh Chloinne Tuireann 50, **51–3**
Oidheadh Chloinne Uisnigh 52
Oisín 1–2
Old Testament 37
Ollam 42–3
Olympus 28
Otherworld, *see also síd(e)* ii, 7–8, 14, 16, 20, 25, 31–4, 50
Partholón 10
Patrick 9, 12–13, 56–7
Philistines 39
Proclus, *Chrestomathy* 28
Psalter, Old Irish treatise on the 34
Qur'ān 18
Ráith Chrúachna, *see also* Crúachan 30, 34, 41
Ráith Murbuilc 13
rechtaire 27
remscél(a) 6, 20–22, 25–6, 59
rudhraigheacht 4
Rudraige mac Sittride 4

—S—
Samain 12, 16, 25
saṃsāra 23
Sanas Cormaic 6, 10, 16, 48
Sárán 45
Scél na Fír Flatha 16, 58
Scél Saltrach na Muicce **46–7**
Sect.o.f.n. 29
Senbecc ua Ebricc 45–6
Senchán Torpéist 48
Serglige Con Culainn 8, 14, 16
Shepherd of Hermas 56
Síd ar Ḟemun, *see also* Síd Ban Find 23
Síd Ban Find, *see also* Síd ar Ḟemun 30, 53–4
Síd Finnachaid 53
Síd in Broga, *see also* Newgrange 20–21
Síd Truim 44
síd(e), *see also* Otherworld iii, 6–12, 14–16, 19, 21–3, 25–7, 29, 31–2, 44, 47, 55–7, 59
Slíab Badbgna 40
Slíab Slánga 13
Smrith 17
Snorri Sturluson 15
Solomon 56
Suibne Geilt 54

—T—
Táin Bó Cúailnge 8, 14, 19–23, 25–7, 32
Táin Bó Fraích 23
Táin Bó Regamna 26, 40
Táin Bó Rúanada 35, 45
tale-lists 3, 5, 38
Tara 6, 32–4, 36–7, 50
Tenga Bithnúa, In 56
Tethra 11
Tigernmas 17
Tír Tairngire 50

Tírechán 9, 16, 57
Titans 10
Tochmarc Baíse Bandruad 45
Tochmarc Becfola 25, **32–4**, 46, 48
Tochmarc Emire 34, 41
Tochmarc Étaíne 6, 10, 14, 20, 27, **29–31**, 32–3, 40, 48, 55, 57
tochomlad(a) 5, 38
Togail Bruidne Da Derga 11, 23, 27, 30, 32–3, 51
Togail Síde Truim 25, **44–5**
Tomus tige Mec ind Óc 39
Tóruigheacht Dhiarmada agus Ghráinne 8, 11
Trí Truagha na Scéalaigheachta 52
Tristan 33
Trojan War 28
Tuarustal nÚadh 42
Túath(a) Dé iii, 7–17, 19, 31–2, 35–6, 38–42, 46, 48–9, 55, 57–9
Túatha Dé Donann 7, 11, 35, 38–9, 42, 49–51, 53, 56
Tuirenn, *see also* Tuirill Picreo 52–3
Tuirill Picreo, *see also* Tuirenn 39, 44, 51
Turnus 49

—U-Z—

Úath Beinne Étair 8
Uí Briúin 27
Uí Néill 6
Ulaid 4, 21–2, 47
Umall 40
Vanir 11, 36
Vergil, *Aeneid* 49
Vita prima Brigitae 57
Zeus 28

Index of Manuscripts

Book of Ballymote 39, 50
Book of Fermoy 46, 51, 56
Book of Leinster 5, 19–20, 22, 42, 44
Chatsworth, Book of Lismore 46
Cín Dromma Snechtai 27
Dublin, NLI MS G 1 39
Dublin, RIA MS 23.E.25; *see* Lebor na hUidre
Dublin, RIA MS 23.E.29; *see* Book of Fermoy
Dublin, RIA MS 23.N.10 35, 39, 45
Dublin, RIA MS 23.O.48; *see* Liber Flavus Fergusiorum
Dublin, RIA MS 23.P.2; *see* Great Book of Lecan
Dublin, RIA MS 23.P.12; *see* Book of Ballymote
Dublin, RIA MS 23.P.16; *see* Leabhar Breac
Dublin, RIA MS 24.P.9 49
Dublin, RIA MS B.iv.1 32
Dublin, RIA MS B.iv.2 39, 47
Dublin, RIA MS D.ii.2 54
Dublin, RIA MS D.iv.2 19, 21, 46
Dublin, TCD MS 1318; *see* Yellow Book of Lecan
Dublin, TCD MS 1319 50
Dublin, TCD MS 1336 35
Dublin, TCD MS 1337 22, 32, 35, 44–6
Dublin, TCD MS 1339; *see* Book of Leinster
Dublin, UCD-OFM MS A 33 50
Edinburgh, National Library of Scotland Adv. MS 72.1.38 53
Great Book of Lecan 51
Leabhar Breac 21
Lebor na hUidre 29
Liber Flavus Fergusiorum 25, 46
London, BL Egerton MS 105 39
London, BL Egerton MS 1781 32
London, BL Egerton MS 1782 20, 22, 25, 30, 33
London, BL Harley MS 5280 17, 25, 34–5, 39, 45, 53
Longford, St Mel's College MS 9 20
Oxford, Bodleian Library, Laud Misc. MS 610 41
Oxford, Bodleian Library, Rawlinson MS B 502 42
Oxford, Bodleian Library, Rawlinson MS B 512 17, 34–5
Yellow Book of Lecan 25, 29–30, 32, 35, 39, 42–3, 47

Index of Scholars

Arbois de Jubainville, H. d' 1–6, 11
Backhaus, N. 20
Baumgarten, R. 5
Bergin, O. 29, 43–4
Best, R.I. 2, 4–5, 29
Bhreathnach, M. 32–3
Blažek, V. 10
Bondarenko, G. 19, 23
Borsje, J. 9
Breatnach, C. 52–4
Breatnach, L. 8
Bruford, A. 48
Carey, J. ii, 5–7, 9–11, 13–15, 25, 30–31, 34–41, 45–6, 51, 55–8
Carney, J. 23, 33–4, 36, 42, 54
Chadwin, T. 20
Charles-Edwards, T. 31
Chesnutt, M. 37
Clarke, M. 11
Clifford, D. 47
Dagger, C. ii, 57
Dahl Hambro, C. 56
de Vries, R. 41, 55
Dillon, M. 2–3, 6–7, 29, 31–2, 34
Dinneen, P.S. 4
Dobbs, M.E. 22, 54–5
Donahue, C. 11
Downey, C. 5
Draak, M. 9
Dröge, Ch. 23
Duignan, L. 8, 26–7
Dumézil, G. 11, 41, 52
Dumville, D.N. 8
Duncan, L. 56–7
Egeler, M. ii
Findon, J. 34
Flahive, J. 4
Fogarty, H. 21, 23
Ford, P.K. 2
Fraser, J. 50
Gray, B. 22
Gray, E. 35–6, 53
Gwynn, E.J. 4
Gwynn, L. 30–31
Hall, A. 15
Hamp, E. 10
Herbert, M. 3
Hollo, K. 44
Hornblower, S. 5
Hoyne, M. 50
Hull, V. 19–20, 25
Johnson, D. 52
Kobel, C. 46
Lehmacher, G. ii
Lévi-Strauss, C. 26
Lewis, C.S. 18
Mac Cana, P. 5
Mac Mathúna, S. ii, 8
MacNeill, M. 13, 55–6
MacQuarrie, C. ii, 48, 56
Maher, M. 19–20
Maier, B. 9
McCone, K. 8, 11, 36–7
McKenna, C. 10
McLaughlin, R. 35–6
Meid, W. 21
Meyer, K. 3, 10, 25
Miller, D.A. 36
Müller-Lisowski, K. 14
Murphy, G. 2–3, 35–6, 50
Murray, K. iii, 20, 24
Ní Bhrolcháin, M. 2
Ó Cathasaigh, T. ii, 3, 6–7, 22, 28, 30, 35
Ó Coileáin, S. 25–6
Ó Corráin, D. iii, 35, 42, 46
Ó Cuív, B. 34, 40, 49
Ó Duilearga, S. 25–6
Ó Flaithearta, M. 25–6
Ó hAodha, T. 40–41
Ó Mainnín, M. 13, 15
Ó Murchadha, D. 40
Pokorny, J. 10, 43
Poppe, E. 3
Puhvel, J. 36
Radner, J. 42
Rees, A. and B. 3

Rodway, S. 11
Roider, U. 22–3
Rose, H.J. 5
Sayers, W. ii, 11
Shaw, F. 20–21
Sims-Williams, P. ii, 34
Sjoestedt, M.-L. 6, 36
Theuerkauf, M. 29
Thurneysen, R. 7, 10, 19–20, 22, 25, 29, 31
Toner, G. 7, 25, 27
Tovar, A. 10
Uther, H.-J. 44, 55
Vendryes, J. 55
Watkins, C. 43
Watson, A. 26
Wiley, D.M. 2, 7
Williams, J.E.C. 2
Williams, M. iii, 9–10, 12, 15–17, 22, 31, 38–9, 42, 53–8

Cork Studies in Celtic Literatures: Publications

1 The Fenian Cycle in Irish and Scots-Gaelic Literature
Joseph Flahive

2 The Case of the Abbot of Drimnagh: A Medieval Irish Story of Sex-Change
Tadhg Ó Síocháin

3 The Mythological Cycle of Medieval Irish Literature
John Carey

Made in United States
North Haven, CT
26 December 2022

30132358R00055